SONNET THEORY AND PRACTICE IN
NINETEENTH-CENTURY FRANCE:
SONNETS ON THE SONNET

University of Hull Publications

Occasional Papers in Modern Languages No. 12

General Editor: Garnet Rees
Professor of French in the
University of Hull

Sonnet Theory and Practice in Nineteenth-century France: Sonnets on the Sonnet

Dᴀᴠɪᴅ H. T. Sᴄᴏᴛᴛ

University of Hull Publications

1977

ISBN 0 85958 408 9
ISSN 0078–3099

Printed in Great Britain by Fretwells Limited
of Hull and London.

CONTENTS

INTRODUCTION

Since Max Jasinski's *Histoire du sonnet en France* of 1903[1], there has been a great lapse in the treatment of the nineteenth-century French sonnet as a subject. This is not to say that critics and exegetes working on nineteenth-century French poetry do not mention or even on occasion discuss the sonnet form, but they never take it up as a subject *per se*. The only exceptions to this rule are provided by sections of books or articles dealing more generally with an author. For example, Claude Cuénot devotes a considerable part of his book *Le Style de Paul Verlaine* (1962) to the sonnet whilst Jean Prévost, in his *Baudelaire* (1953) gives us what is perhaps the most interesting single study treating a nineteenth-century poet's use of the sonnet since Albert Cassagne's *Versification et métrique de Charles Baudelaire* of 1906[2]. However, as our bibliography illustrates, studies as useful as these latter are extremely few and far between.

This lapse in the treatment of the nineteenth-century French sonnet becomes serious in view of the fact that the few extensive works on the French sonnet that do exist, partly owing to their age, no longer give an adequate survey or analysis of the subject. Jasinski, for example, gives an excellent survey of the sonnet up to Baudelaire, but thereafter his grasp of significant developments in the form becomes seriously impaired. Preferring the Parnassians to the Symbolists (the study is dedicated to Heredia 'noble poète des *Trophées'*) Jasinski devotes more space to Samain than to Mallarmé (whom, moreover, he scarcely mentions) and has nothing at all to say about Corbière and Laforgue as sonneteers.

This absence of critical study appears even more deplorable when it is seen how many important later nineteenth-century poets had recourse to the form. Here again, poets like Corbière and Laforgue have been unduly neglected. And although, more recently, many articles have been written on the more esoteric or hermetic 'Symbolist' sonnets—such as Nerval's *El Desdichado* or Mallarmé's *Sonnet en —yx*—these poems have almost invariably been treated in isolation: there has seldom been any real attempt to assess the more general significance of the nineteenth-century poet's use of the sonnet.

In an article entitled 'L'Esthétique valéryenne du sonnet', Jean Hytier remarks that:

> Il y aurait une petite étude à faire sur les comparaisons auxquelles le sonnet a donné lieu, et, en particulier, celles qu'on trouve dans les *sonnets sur le sonnet* . . .'3

The aim of this short study, in part, is to fill this gap but not merely in a way sufficient to satisfy a dilettante's curiosity about minor verse forms. For as we have suggested and as we hope more fully to show, in the history of nineteenth-century French poetry, the sonnet plays a central role. In attempting to terminate the long neglect of the nineteenth-century French sonnet we shall, therefore, at the same time, try to reassert its fundamental importance as a poetic phenomenon.

To consider nineteenth-century French sonnets on the sonnet without attempting to relate them to a broader context, both theoretical and practical, would be otiose: it would be a study of literary curiosities, not an exploration of an important trend in the development of nineteenth-century French poetry. It is for this reason that the concept of the 'sonnet on the sonnet' is taken as a point of departure rather than as the *subject* of the following study. Although, with the notable exception of Baudelaire, nearly all the great sonneteers of the century attempted this sort of poem in one form or another, not all of them did so explicitly. The 1868 version of Mallarmé's *Ses purs ongles* . . . (then entitled *Sonnet allégorique de lui-même)* is very much a sonnet on the sonnet in disguise whilst Nerval's sonnet *Epitaphe* and Laforgue's sonnet *Apothéose* only allude to the sonnet and in a way that takes on real depth only in the broader context of these poet's sonnet development as a whole. Meanwhile, those sonneteers who, with the important exception of Corbière and Gautier, write explicit sonnets on the sonnet (and this applies particularly to the minor and very often provincial sonneteers like Boulay-Paty, Brizeux and Soulary) on the whole tend to do so in the spirit of a game or a party-piece rather than as an effort towards defining the fundamental nature and tendencies of the sonnet as they see it. Soulary's *Le Sonnet,* for example, gives only vague intimations of the poet's reasons for a more general use of the form (Soulary being one of the most prolific sonneteers of the century); it does not embody, as Mallarmé's *Sonnet allégorique de lui-même* will, the very processes the poet will consistently apply in his mature sonnet development. Meanwhile, Baudelaire, who wrote no specific sonnets on the sonnet, is one of the poets in whom we see an original pattern of the sonnet developing perhaps more clearly than in any other poet of the century except Mallarmé. Since, given this fact, it would be inconceivable for this study to eschew Baudelaire, we shall go into his development of the sonnet in some detail. In doing so, however, we shall attempt, as far as possible, to relate it both to his theoretical ideas on the sonnet (in themselves some of the most incisive and revelatory of the century) and to the influence these ideas had, through his sonnet practice, on the next generation and particularly on those poets who contributed to *Le Parnasse contemporain* of 1866. One of these poets, Arsène Houssaye, as we shall see, in a sense writes Baudelaire's sonnet on the sonnet for him; for Houssaye's *Les Quatre Saisons* exemplifies many of the most characteristic tendencies of the Baudelairian sonnet.

The principal aim of this study becomes thus not simply an historical survey of the nineteenth-century French sonnet on the sonnet but an attempt to explain fundamental sonnet developments in relation to sonnet theory throughout the century. The concept of the sonnet on the sonnet is used and elaborated therefore primarily as a means of bringing into focus, in a short study, questions concerning nineteenth-century sonnet development of a broader nature, questions, for example, of the following kind:

  (i) What was the nature in France of the nineteenth-century revival of the sonnet and who were its first exponents?

 (ii) To what extent does a theory of the sonnet develop throughout the century and how closely does it reflect sonnet-writing in practice?

(iii) Why was it that the sonnet form was exploited with particular originality by 'Symbolist' poets like Nerval, Baudelaire and Mallarmé?

 (iv) What fluctuations in attitude towards the sonnet are perceptible as the century develops?

As the above programme implies, in the survey that follows, more space is devoted to the 'Symbolist'[4] sonneteers than the 'Parnassians'. Nerval, Baudelaire and Mallarmé each have a section to themselves whilst their respective contemporaries—Gautier, Leconte de Lisle and Heredia—are grouped together in the one chapter on the Parnassian sonnet. This is not meant in any way to depreciate the importance of the Parnassians as sonneteers or to imply that Leconte de Lisle and Heredia were not capable of great things in this form. It is merely to suggest that the Parnassian poets tended to explore the potential of the sonnet along fairly common lines. We shall point out, in Chapter II, the striking similarity of Gautier's and Banville's sonnet theories and although it is true that Gautier took the sonnet some way towards the developments that later Symbolist sonneteers (and especially Baudelaire) were to realise with some consistency, thereafter he and his younger Parnassian associates tended, in spite of continued experiments with rhyme, to concentrate on consolidating rather than exploring further the sonnet's potential. This is clearly seen in their general unwillingness, in their poetry, to relax the descriptive or discursive reins and consciously allow images the greater degree of autonomy they begin to enjoy, for example, in some of Baudelaire's sonnets. As W. Mönch suggests, having affirmed the importance of Gautier in the early stages of nineteenth-century French sonnet development: 'la libération du sonnet se fit avec Baudelaire.'[5]

But this is not the only reason why the Symbolist poets as sonneteers are given priority over the Parnassians. As we have already noted, the last survey of the nineteenth-century sonnet with any claim to comprehensiveness—that of Jasinski—does the Parnassian sonneteers fairly full justice but almost entirely neglects the Symbolist sonneteers after Baudelaire. One function of this study is therefore to redress this balance. Secondly, it seems fair to claim that for no Parnassian sonneteer except Heredia did the sonnet play the central role that it played in the poetry of Nerval, Baudelaire and Mallarmé. In Gautier's 'recueil capital' *Emaux et camées* (1852) there is only one sonnet (and this the *Préface*); *Poèmes barbares* (1862–72) is the only published collection of Leconte de Lisle's poems that includes more than a handful of sonnets; and for Banville, as a glance at the contents of his complete works will show, the sonnet was only one of many fixed forms offering scope for his astounding technical virtuosity. Turning to the Symbolist poets, the picture is rather different. Nerval's major contribution to nineteenth-century French poetry—*Les Chimères* (1854)—consists entirely of sonnets whilst half the poems in Baudelaire's *Les Fleurs du Mal* are in this form; and almost all of Mallarmé's poetry in verse written after 1873 takes the form of the sonnet.

Our feeling of the *individual* importance of the contribution of some Symbolist sonneteers is of course strengthened by their often highly individualistic but nonetheless far-reaching theoretical interest in the sonnet form—one that finds expression as much in their letters and comments to friends as in more general treatises or *partis pris*. Here again, the difference between the Parnassians and the Symbolists as sonneteers is clear. With the former, as we have already implied, there seems to have been a more general acceptance of aims and a common effort towards their realisation than with the latter. It is also, therefore, partly for this reason that certain Symbolist sonneteers are given separate treatment.

The grouping of Verlaine, Corbière and Laforgue under one heading, though with a separate sub-section for each, is perhaps easier to justify; for in 'The Ironic Line' we observe highly individualistic attitudes towards later nineteenth-century sonnet developments and yet ones closely related by the common bond of Irony. Although there are other sonneteers who might have been represented here—for example, the rather neglected Charles Cros (1842–1888)—their inclusion would have offered further illustration rather than a new dimension to the argument. The same is not true of Valéry however whom we briefly mention in our closing chapter but whose sonnet theory and practice we do not develop fully in in this study. Strictly speaking, the Valéry of *Charmes* (1922) is a twentieth-century poet and the restricted space of this study has obliged us to let him remain so, even though some of his early sonnets (in 1920 collected in the *Album de vers anciens*) and his early theoretical remarks (for example, his letter to Pierre Louÿs of 2 June 1890), not to mention his general literary tastes and attitudes, root him quite firmly in the nineteenth century. Since, however, these and other considerations relating to Valéry are touched on in our Conclusion, we take them no further here.

One would like to be able to give a full account of the theory and development of the French sonnet before the nineteenth century but this would be beyond the scope of this study and might, in any case, duplicate work that has already been done in this field.[6] Nevertheless, a few words about the general nature and origins of the sonnet in France might not be amiss. The modern French sonnet has its origins in the fourteenth-century Italian sonnet and finds its first expression in the first half of the sixteenth century. Clémont Marot and Mellin de Saint-Gelais were the first poets to compose sonnets in French.[7] The structure of the regular French sonnet is largely based on that of Petrarch: the *abba abba* rhyme-scheme of the octave was inherited unchanged from the Italian, only the disposition of the sestet rhymes showing some variation, the *ccd ede* or *ccd eed* scheme most commonly superseding the Italian *cdc dcd* or *cde cde* (though other irregular patterns were also common).

The French and Italian sonnet tradition is, of course, quite different from the English. The Elizabethan sonnet, the form used by Shakespeare, is a 'quatorzain' terminating in a rhyming couplet: the way it works has really very little in common with the Franco-Italian sonnet. For one of the chief characteristics of the latter is the built-in reminder of its thirteenth-century origins in the fusion of the Italian *strambotto* and the Sicilian *sextine*,[8] two formal units in, respectively, eight and six alternating rhymes. In a sense the continental (as opposed to the English) sonnet has always been a poem in two parts and successive sonneteers have mostly sought to preserve the different character of each, with the result that the change or 'turn' from one formal unit to the other, from the octave to the sestet, has always been a significant one. Part of Petrarch's genius as a sonneteer lies in the way in which, by standardizing the use of 'embraced' rhymes in the octave and by often introducing a third rhyme into the sestet, he enhances the individual character of the sonnet's two parts. In a way, the more the separate formal units of the sonnet are emphasized, the more sonnet-like the sonnet becomes and it may well be because of this that the 'Petrarchan' form of the sonnet (of the octave, at least) has, outside England, established itself as the standard form. For this reason, it is perhaps important, as far as possible, for the poet to adhere to the characteristic 'embraced' rhymes of the sonnet octave, for, in doing so, not only does he set up a pattern of some lyrical intensity and distinction but also makes this pattern itself contrast more effectively with the sestet's different rhyme-scheme.

This must not be taken to imply that the 'sonnetness' of the sonnet necessarily *depends* on its 'regularity', for this is not the case. Baudelaire, for example, like some of the Pléiade poets, often used 'irregular' rhyme-schemes in his sonnets but, in spite of what Heredia will say (as we shall see), they were nonetheless sonnets and successful ones at that, and this because their rhyme-schemes continued to create specific and appropriately sonnet-like effects. Baudelaire's 'irregular' sonnets were not accidents but deliberate and interesting *variations* on the form. The sixteenth-century French sonnet is itself a variation on the fourteenth-century Italian sonnet and at no point in its long European career can it be said that the sonnet has been *absolutely* fixed. However, a concept of regularity is useful in that it may help us to account for certain sorts of ir-regularity, put us in a better position to answer the question: what does this irregularity bring with it to justify the deviation from the norm? For true originality as a sonneteer—and this applies as much to the sonnet as to other fixed forms, indeed is part of the reason why they have become more or less *fixed*—expresses itself less perhaps through flagrant divergence from the norm than through a kind of incontrovertible manifestation of its necessity. Unlike the whimsical Musset then, whose sonnet irregularities simply weaken even further an already tenuous and desultory treatment of the sonnet structure, and unlike the refractory Verlaine who will consistently attempt, at one stage in his career, to assert his originality as a sonneteer through transgression, the sonneteer of genius, a Mallarmé for example, will assert himself not through trespassing but through supererogation: by his use not only of regular but of ultra-rich rhymes, at the same time contriving to make even these latter seem absolutely required by the poem.

I

THE NINETEENTH-CENTURY REVIVAL OF THE SONNET

'Un sonnet sans défauts vaut seul un long poëme'[1]

The revival of the nineteenth-century French sonnet did not coincide with the great revival of nineteenth-century French poetry by the Romantics in the early 1820s. The reasons for this are fairly easy to see. The Romantic poets' first priorities tended towards liberating French poetry from the conventions that a poetically rather sterile eighteenth century had inherited, largely uncritically, from the one which preceded it. The greater rhythmic flexibility that Lamartine, Hugo and Vigny sought, involving a more expansive use of the alexandrine in which *enjambement* and a mobile caesura had a crucial role to play, did not seem to them to be particularly compatible with strict forms like the sonnet (although, as later poets were to demonstrate—Baudelaire, for example, in his sonnet *La Musique*—rhythmic flexibility and a strict form are by no means incompatible). But the early Romantics' thematic ambitions also inevitably exerted here a profound influence on their verse's formal direction. For the verse line of the French Romantics seemed initially to be the natural complement to the long poem in which the poet's "large-limbed visions"[2] found their fullest expression. Having made a debut with longish lyrics—as in Lamartine's *Premières Méditations* of 1820 or Hugo's odes of the early 1820s—their maturity is characterized by poems that become increasingly epic in their themes and proportions—Lamartine's *Jocelyn* (1836) and *La Chute d'un ange* (1838), Hugo's *La Légende des siècles* (1859 and after) and *La Fin de Satan* (1886). As Jasinski affirms of Lamartine, Vigny and Hugo:

> tous trois se ressemblaient par leur dédain de la symétrie extérieure, leur prédilection pour les grands morceaux simples de plans et de lignes. Leurs lectures étaient les épopées antiques et étrangères; ils admiraient le lyrisme étincelant et barbare des prophètes . . . et le sonnet devait leur paraître méprisable.[3]

In this context, it is easy to see why the short poem was not recognized as being a particularly favourable medium. It had neither the space, time nor impetus for the sustained enterprises of the Romantic poet. Because it had little leisure and no stamina, it could not do justice to the historical or descriptive subject matter of the epic. It is for this reason that in France the long poem naturally became the Romantic poem *par excellence*.

In spite of this, the first great Romantics do, unwittingly in a sense, prepare for the sonnet's revival. For the modification in the form of French verse that Hugo, for example, had been instrumental in bringing about—the shifting of the caesura and the weakening, through *enjambement*, of the tonic stress which had always accompanied the last unmuted syllable of the French verse line—had been accompanied by a renewed interest in rhyme. As Becq de Fouquières affirms:

> C'est la rime qui, précisément, assure la liberté du rythme. Aussi, à mesure que le rythme se complique, que les éléments rythmiques se combinent suivant des rapports de plus en plus éloignées, la rime au contraire, tend à devenir de plus en plus riche et exacte. Nous verrons cette loi se vérifier quand nous étudierons le vers romantique.[4]

One effect of this new interest was that the austere range of classical rhymes was vastly enlarged and enriched in French Romantic verse and this, in a sense, paved the way for the sonnet, a form whose expressive power depends very considerably on the richness and variety of its rhymes. The result was that, by the 1840s, the cult of rich rhyme, which in the following extract Wilhem Ténint sees as being one of the French Romantics' great achievements, also came to be an inseparable part of sonnet composition:

> La nouvelle école . . . a rendu à la rime son importance et sa valeur; elle a professé hautement le culte de la rime riche, culte depuis longtemps oublié.[5]

It is also interesting to note that the first great nineteenth-century French sonneteer is not Sainte-Beuve (1804–1869) who, as we shall presently see, rescued the sonnet from the oblivion of over a century, but Gautier who, in a sense, became susceptible to the sonnet only perhaps through his initial susceptibility to the rich rhymes and formal perfection of Hugo's *Les Orientales* (1829), a collection in which there were, of course, no sonnets. For in the 1830s, Gautier applied a technical expertise as dazzling as Hugo's to the cultivation of the sonnet itself rather than to the longer poems that Hugo, on the whole, continued to favour.

Although, then, certain aspects of the early development of French Romantic poetry indirectly prepared for the sonnet's revival, these did not make the task of the innovator any less awkward. That Sainte-Beuve was aware of the relevance of the Romantics' revival of rich rhyme to a revival of the short poem is shown in the following comment on Ronsard's technique in *De l'élection de son sépulcre*:

> il a très bien compris qu'à une si courte distance une grande richesse de rime était indispensable, et il s'est montré ici plus rigoureux sur ce point qu'à son ordinaire. C'est en effet une loi de notre versification que, plus les rimes correspondantes se rapprochent, plus elles doivent être riches et complètes.[6]

And the second poem in the *Poésies de Joseph Delorme* (1829), called *A la rime*, explores both the formal and the suggestive possibilities of rhyme. But this did not make Sainte-Beuve any less cautious in his desire to revive interest in formal or technical matters for their own sake, matters around which discussion of the sonnet often tended to revolve. The reasons for this cautiousness are again easy to see. For to take an open interest in formal detail at a time when thematic ambitions dominated in poetry, when a variable caesura and *enjambement* were employed not so much for their own sake as to help expand the poets rhythmical muscles, was to risk laying oneself open to ridicule—as the mixed irony and embarrassment of Sainte-Beuve's following remark clearly illustrates:

> Sans doute en ce siècle de haute philosophie, de lumineuse émotion et de grave politique, beaucoup de ces fines remarques, de ces confidences techniques à propos d'une chanson ou d'un sonnet, pourront d'abord sembler futiles et ridicules.[7]

It is hardly surprising therefore to find that, even within the broad scope of the *Tableau historique et critique de la poésie française au XVI siècle* of 1828, there is, apart from the rare observations already cited, relatively little discussion of the formal techniques of the sonneteer. Again, this is because Sainte-Beuve, in the nineteenth-century context we have just described, falls shy of placing 'bel esprit' above lyrical vigour, as the following passage from the *Tableau* seems to suggest:

> Le sonnet qu'on va lire [Vauquelin de la Fresnaie's *O vent plaisant*] est du petit nombre de ceux où le sentiment triomphe du bel esprit, où la forme

donne du relief au sentiment, et desquels on serait tenté de dire sans épigramme qu'ils *valent un long poëme.*[8]

Sainte-Beuve's reticence here is not mere pusillanimity for even in mid-century we see Barbey d'Aurevilly, reviewing Soulary's *Sonnets humoristiques* (1858), expressing, in an exaggerated manner, the kind of virile impatience with trifles that Sainte-Beuve, perhaps unnecessarily, feared to a certain extent in his great Romantic contemporaries:

> Ah! le plus beau de tout, c'est la grandeur dans l'être, c'est l'étendue dans la forme puissante, c'est l'ampleur dans le geste humain! Que les faiseurs de sonnets et les tailleurs de petits cristaux ou de petits cailloux le sachent bien! Ils ne viennent jamais que les seconds ou que les troisièmes. Qu'est Benvenuto en comparaison de Michel-Ange! Combien les plus beaux poèmes épiques ont-ils de chants?[9]

Sainte-Beuve's initial attitude to the sonnet therefore is a guarded one: he does not announce the revival of the sonnet as a panacea for the poet but reintroduces it almost apologetically:

> Ne ris point des sonnets, ô Critique moqueur!
> Par amour autrefois en fit le grand Shakspeare;
> C'est sur ce luth heureux que Pétrarque soupire,
> Et que le Tasse aux fers soulage un peu son cœur;
>
> Camoens de son exil abrège la longueur,
> Car il chante en sonnets l'amour et son empire;
> Dante aime cette fleur de myrte, et la respire,
> Et la mêle au cyprès qui ceint son front vainqueur;
>
> Spencer, s'en revenant de l'île des féeries,
> Exhale en longs sonnets ses tristesses chéries;
> Milton, chantant les siens, ranimait son regard;
>
> Moi, je veux rajeunir le doux sonnet en France;
> Du Bellay, le premier, l'apporta de Florence,
> Et l'on en sait plus d'un de notre vieux Ronsard.

This sonnet on the sonnet, the century's first, is not so much about the sonnet as a form as about its great and historic exponents and the kind of *subjects* they tended to develop within the sonnet framework. It was of course inspired by Wordsworth's *Scorn not the sonnet* (1827) and since the influence of the English sonnet tradition on Sainte-Beuve's revival of the sonnet in France was crucial, it is interesting, very briefly, to compare developments in the two countries.

In the first place, the English sonnet tradition after the Renaissance had always been stronger than the French. After the Pléiade and throughout the seventeeth century, the sonnet in France became increasingly discredited in spite both of its occasional sensational popularity (whether in the salons of the first half of the century or in the 'Querelle à propos de Job et d'Uranie' of 1649) and of its strong theoretical support by writers as different as Colletet (whose *Traité du sonnet* appeared in 1658) and Boileau in his *Art poétique* (1674, from which this chapter's epigraph is taken). Whilst in France the sonnet was going into decline, in the England of roughly the same period, Milton was infusing the English sonnet with renewed vigour and purity and in doing so reverted to a form that more nearly resembled the Petrarchan original than the seven-rhyme sonnet most commonly cultivated by the Elizabethans. Similarly, whereas in eighteenth-century France the sonnet had almost completely disappeared from the scene, in England it was, towards the end of the century, already being revived by Bowles—a poet who was later to be imitated by both Wordsworth and Sainte-Beuve. Except for a lean period at the beginning of the eighteenth-century then, the sonnet had always been taken seriously by English poets and its revival at the beginning of the nineteenth century was easily achieved. This, as we have seen, was not the case with the French Romantics who had a far broader gap of years to bridge before they could re-establish contact with their own sonnet tradition in its vigorous sixteenth-century prime.

In the second place, English Romantic poets differ significantly from the French Romantics in that they sometimes showed themselves to be as interested in the short as in the long poem. For as well as being great epic poets Wordsworth and Keats, for example (both of whose sonnets were imitated by Sainte-Beuve), were also highly self-conscious sonneteers[10]—see for example Keats' subtle sonnet *On the Sonnet* (1819) and Wordsworth's *Prefatory Sonnet* (1807) and *Scorn not the Sonnet* (1827). However, it was not so much the sophistication and self-consciousness of these two poets as sonneteers that appealed to Sainte-Beuve (there were a number of self-conscious French sonneteers of the sixteenth- and seventeenth-centuries who would have satisfied him on that count) as their *subject matter*. For rather than restrict themselves to the idealising

Petrarchan tradition, the nineteenth-century English poets, writing in a far more various, even miscellaneous sonnet tradition, would adapt the sonnet to any theme, but more particularly, and this applies above all to Wordsworth, to the romantic description of Nature. It was thus by imitating the varied subject matter of the English Romantic sonneteers as much as letting himself become influenced by the technical ingenuity of the French poets of the Pléiade that Sainte-Beuve hoped to make his revival of the sonnet a more viable proposition in the context of the French Romantic poetry of the 1820s. It remains to be seen whether his attempts were successful.

Enid Hamer wrote of Wordsworth:

> No poet ever wrote so many sonnets as Wordsworth, and few great poets were so seldom visited by a genuine sonnet inspiration. The number of really great sonnets from his massive collections would form an even smaller group than Milton's. As he travelled anywhere, by night or by day, on foot or by coach, Wordsworth's mind seems to have been perpetually cogitating sonnets . . . The habit may have been caught from Bowles, and it is not a good one, for the simple description of a scene or incident is seldom fitly set forth as a sonnet.[11]

and this criticism is one that could with equal justice be levelled at Sainte-Beuve, for he too was 'seldom visited by a genuine sonnet inspiration'. Although Sainte-Beuve, in by far the larger portion of his hundred-odd sonnets, uses the standard Petrarchan rhyme-scheme (the *abba abba* octave followed by a sestet in *ccd eed* or *ccd ede,* forms used most often by Ronsard and the other poets of the Pléiade), his handling of a potentially complex and subtle structure is remarkably simplified.[12] Little of its potential suggestiveness is exploited and there is little contribution to the development of its form. In spite of the interesting and subtle theoretical poem *A la rime*, which appears towards the beginning of the *Poésies de Joseph Delorme,* in which both the technical:

Rime, qui donnes leurs sons
   Aux chansons,
Rime, l'unique harmonie
Du vers, qui, sans tes accents,
   Frémissants,
Serait muet au génie . . .

and almost mystical:

> Clef, qui, loin de l'œil mortel,
>   Sur l'autel
> Ouvres l'arche du miracle;
> Ou tiens le vase embaumé
>   Renfermé
> Dans le cèdre au tabernacle . . .

qualities of rhyme are recognized, when Sainte-Beuve in practice turns to the sonnet form, his exploitation of rhyme is almost invariably unmemorable. As Ferdinand Brunetière declares:

> Cette imagination de la rime qu'il a lui-même si bien chantée. Sainte-Beuve ne l'a pas eue.[13]

L'Amant antiquaire, for example, is a sonnet, inspired by Petrarch, in which rhymes tend to match the phonetic with the grammatical, the masculine noun with the masculine noun, the imperfect verb with the imperfect verb, and so on:

> De l'étude où je vais ne prends point jalousie;
> Ne la crois pas surtout rivale de l'amour.
> J'entre en ces parchemins et j'épelle alentour,
> Cherchant l'esprit des morts sous la page moisie.
>
> Pétrarque, notre maître à tous en poésie,
> Chers aux dévots amants dont il conduit la Cour,
> Ne faisait, Laure à part, qu'assembler, rendre au jour
> Mainte docte relique, à propos ressaisie.
>
> Il portait, sais-tu bien? dans son secret réduit,
> Non pas l'habit de pourpre, où, de loin, il nous luit
> Depuis qu'au Capitole il reçut sa couronne,
>
> Mais une veste en cuir, où vite il écrivait,
> Sur les bords et partout, sitôt qu'il le trouvait,
> Beau mot cicéronien, ou beau vers de canzone.

The 'amour'/'Cour'/'jour' rhyme is an especially banal one: it appears, in the plural, in the sonnet *Attendre, attendre encore* only two pages before. Here Gide's criticism of Ronsard might with far greater justice be directed against Sainte-Beuve:

> il se contente vite et rime négligemment, fiançant des vocables de même formation et . . . qui ne satisfont que trop facilement l'oreille sans apporter quoi que ce soit de surprenant et de hardi . . . C'est méconnaître le ravissement causé par l'inattendu rapprochement de mots étrangers l'un à l'autre et par le tour de force de l'esprit qui parvient à les accointer . . .[14]

Sainte-Beuve's concern for the sonnet did, however, have two important results. The first was that of reintroducing the sonnet into a context that was otherwise largely dominated by the long poem; and the second, that of bringing the sonnet to the notice of contemporary poets as an authentic modern poetic form, capable of adaptation to a modern subject matter and yet that, at the same time, reunited them to a French poetic tradition. The twelfth 'pensée' of *Joseph Delorme* expresses a dawning theoretical recognition of the sonnet form's potentialities that, for the time, was quite prophetic. It prefigures that crucial moment of metamorphosis in nineteenth-century French poetry in which the poet, achieving a complete transformation of his technique, turns from the long poem to the concise and concentrated verses that were later to become so characteristic of the Symbolist sonneteers:

> Tel filet d'idée poétique qui, chez André Chénier, découlerait en élégie, ou chez Lamartine s'épancherait en méditation, et finirait par devenir fleuve ou lac, se congèle aussitôt chez moi, et se cristallise en sonnet; c'est un malheur et je m'y résigne.
> —Une idée dans un sonnet, c'est une goutte d'essence dans une larme de cristal.

There can be little doubt that Sainte-Beuve's influence on Baudelaire was direct, as the following couplet from an early poem dedicated by the latter poet to the former confirms:

> Ce fut dans ce conflit de molles circonstances,
> Mûri par vos sonnets, préparé par vos stances . . .[15]

Before moving on to Gautier and to the discussion of sonnet developments in the 1830s, a brief mention must be made of Musset (1810–1857) as a sonneteer. Although most of Musset's sonnets were composed in the later 1830s and in the 1840s, they do not reflect any of the more 'Parnassian' tendencies that Gautier's and Banville's early sonnets of the same period begin to manifest. Musset's first sonnet *(Que j'aime le premier frisson d'hiver! . . .)* was composed as early as 1829, when the poet was still in his teens, but as he matured, Musset's development of the sonnet did not seem to follow any regular or consistent pattern or attempt to achieve any new aims. Indeed, for the most part, Musset's slender and nonchalant selection of sonnets are very much poems in a light or casual vein. Much more than Sainte-Beuve, Musset seems to have used the sonnet as a kind of graceful, even nostalgic, but fundamentally inconsequential form to which the poet reverted when he had neither the energy nor the inclination to write a longer poem. When Musset writes, somewhat parenthetically, in the second quatrain of the third in a trio of sonnets sent in 1843 to Charles Nodier's daughter Marie, Mme. Ménessier:

> Bonjour, ami sonnet, si doux, si bienveillant,
> Poésie, amitié que le vulgaire ignore,
> Gentil bouquet de fleurs, de larmes tout brillant,
> Que dans un noble cœur un soupir fait éclore...

he is expressing not so much a theory of the sonnet as a kind of whimsical delight in its form—a form, however, whose finer details he made little attempt to study. As Jean Prévost remarks:

> Musset ne compose de sonnets qu'aux heures lentes ou oisives, pour encadrer quelques vers auxquels sa pensée ni son émotion n'ont plus rien à ajouter.[16]

and the following line from the sonnet *Le Fils du Titien* (1838):

> J'ai le cœur de Pétrarque et n'ai point son génie

sums up both Musset's own position vis à vis the sonnet and also to a certain extent that of Sainte-Beuve whose sonnet theory or intentions were never quite fulfilled in practice.

II

GAUTIER AND THE PARNASSIAN SONNET

The history of the nineteenth-century French sonnet's development becomes more complex in the 1830s. As well as Sainte-Beuve
and Musset, Auguste Barbier (1805–1882), whose *Il Pianto*, con-
taining ten sonnets, appeared in 1833, and Félix Arvers (1806–1851),
to name but two, were beginning to experiment with the sonnet
form, the latter's *Sonnet imité de l'Italien,* dedicated (like Musset's
sonnets mentioned above), to Nodier's daughter Marie, enjoying
for a while considerable celebrity (it appeared in *Mes Heures
perdues* of 1833). But rather than these, it is Gautier's sonnets of the
1830s that really set the pattern for later sonnet developments by
both Parnassian and Symbolist poets. For if Sainte-Beuve's *Joseph
Delorme* had supplied the theoretical inspiration for the future
master sonneteer, Gautier (1811–1872) provided more tangible
illustrations, particularly in the field of technique. For Gautier's
sonnets embody, *avant la lettre,* the Parnassian swing towards the
exploitation of the objective qualities of verse and show a specific
preoccupation with the formal qualities of the sonnet, its shape,
elegance and concision. It is thus Gautier rather than Sainte-
Beuve who becomes the true father of the nineteenth-century French
sonnet amongst whose progeny Baudelaire, Mallarmé, Heredia and
even Valéry may be counted.

Gautier was really the first great purist of the century. His
'purism' was far from being purely academic however. Although, on
the one hand, his sonnets are formally purer than Musset's, they
are also, on the other, more imaginative than those correct but
unaudacious poems of Sainte-Beuve. Out of a total of seventy-two
sonnets, sixty-six use the Petrarchan octave rhyme-scheme. The
octave of Sainte-Beuve's sonnet was, as we saw, equally regular,
but Gautier seems to have been the first important French poet of
the century to exploit more fully its suggestive potential. Baudelaire
himself, who in *Les Fleurs du Mal* manages a regular Petrarchan
octave only on ten occasions (out of over seventy), was criticized by
Gautier for his 'sonnets libertins, c'est-à-dire, non orthodoxes et
s'affranchissant volontiers de la quadruple rime.'[1] For Gautier's
experiments with the sonnet, anticipating those of the mature

Mallarmé, never destroy the inherent shape of the classical sonnet. Indeed, the attitude of the 'parfait magicien ès lettres françaises' to the sonnet is a masterpiece of ironical respect:

> Il faut . . . se soumettre absolument à ses lois, ou bien, si l'on trouve ses lois surannées, pédantesques et gênantes, ne pas écrire de sonnets du tout.[2]

Instead of tinkering with the rhyme-scheme in the rather whimsical and ineffectual fashion of a Musset, or drastically altering it as Baudelaire on occasion will, Gautier sets out to explore the essential qualities of its original form.

Like Banville, Heredia and Mallarmé, Gautier recognized that the *point de départ* of the sonnet is rhyme. In his exploitation of it, as his experiments with *bouts rimés*[3] confirm, he is far more ambitious than Sainte-Beuve. A true Parnassian, he was early to recognize the expressive potential of *rime rare*. However, the boldness of rhyme juxtaposition in Gautier's later sonnets seems to imply a deliberate parody of rhyme. Note, for example, the linking of 'Danemark' and 'Bismark', 'Crac' and 'trac' in *Nous voilà réunis* and 'tempère' and 'Ampère', 'Lancret' and 'vaincrait' in *Estelle*[4]. Displaying a virtuosity reminiscent of seventeenth-century rhymers, Gautier creates, in the *Hippogriffes* of the *Bouts rimés* series, two different sonnets on the basis of an identical rhyme-scheme. Similarly, although Gautier's experiments with acrostics—for example, the acrostic sonnet *Estelle Gautier*—are not serious poetry[5], they nevertheless reveal preoccupations comparable, though less subtle and serious, with those of Nerval in his sonnet *Horus*.

This rapid survey of Gautier's treatment of the sonnet form must not in itself be taken as a proof of the primacy of his influence on the great nineteenth-century sonneteers. For although Nerval and Baudelaire started writing sonnets after Gautier, he subsequently outlived both of them. Most of the great Baudelairian and Nervalian poems antedated (and no doubt considerably influenced) Gautier's later sonnets, particularly the more overtly experimental ones that we have been discussing, nearly all of which were written in the 1860s when the French sonnet was at the height of its vogue. And Gautier's sonnet on the sonnet, to be analysed presently, was not written until 1870, by which time Gautier must have been acquainted not only with the sonnets of Nerval and Baudelaire but also with the early efforts of Mallarmé and Verlaine in this form. This does not however necessarily reduce Gautier's originality as a sonneteer, since a small group of early sonnets written between 1833 and 1838 already offered a new and influential contribution to the sonnet form[6]. For it was amongst these poems that the sonnet, anticipating by nearly a decade the achievements of Nerval and Baudelaire, emerges as a new and sophisticated poetic phenomenon.

A detailed analysis of one of these sonnets more than adequately reveals the debt of a sonneteer like Baudelaire to Gautier. It would be difficult to dispute for example the originality of the sonnet *A deux beaux yeux:*

Vous avez un regard singulier et charmant;
Comme la lune au fond du lac qui la reflète,
Votre prunelle, où brille une humide paillette,
Au coin de vos doux yeux roule languissamment.

Ils semblent avoir pris ses feux au diamant;
Ils sont de plus belle eau qu'une perle parfaite,
Et vos grands cils émus, de leur aile inquiète
Ne voilent qu'à demi leur vif rayonnement.

Mille petits amours à leur miroir de flamme
Se viennent regarder et s'y trouvent plus beaux
Et les désirs y vont rallumer leurs flambeaux.

Ils sont si transparents qu'ils laissent voir votre âme,
Comme une fleur céleste au calice idéal
Que l'on apercevrait à travers un cristal.

The poem takes the form of a celebration in the Petrarchan manner of a loved object whose beauty and mysteriousness are expressed in one of those graceful but provocative paradoxes the technique of which Baudelaire was directly to inherit. The whole of the rest of the octave enlarges upon the initial image whose suggestive qualities are reincarnated in further images themselves richly suggestive. The eyes 'regard' alternatively expands to become the reflection of the moon on the lake or contracts to become the moist spangle, 'l'humide paillette', in the centre of the pupil, analogies that constitute optical variations on the same fundamental image.

Avoiding the monotonous grammatical rhyme to which Sainte-

Beuve often had recourse, Gautier, in the first quatrain of the sonnet, makes each rhyme word a different part of speech, a sequence of adjective, verb, noun, adverb. Just as the second quatrain reflects the rhymes of the first, its imagery attempts to bring into focus the variations of the first. The moon's reflection in the lake (l. 2) becomes, in its formal equivalent (l. 2 of the second quatrain), crystallized into the 'perle parfaite', whilst the eyes of the first quatrain have, in the second, taken on a diamond-like quality. Similarly, just as the 'prunelle' of the first quatrain regulated the brilliance of the 'humide paillette', the 'grands cils émus' of the second quatrain control in a differently expressive way the eyes' 'vif rayonnement'.

The octave as a whole thus gives complex expression to a movement of objective, quasi-scientific observation that is fused with an emotional reaction that becomes increasingly intense. Both modes of perception, the minute, almost microscopic play of light in the loved one's eyes and the lyrical idealisation that gives them their emotional resonance, are perfectly synthesized in the two balanced quatrains with their reciprocity of rhyme-scheme and imagery.

The regular Petrarchan octave is contrasted with an irregular sestet. Unlike Sainte-Beuve, whose adherence to the conventional *ccd ede* or *ccd eed* sestet was remarkable in its consistency if not in its brilliance, Gautier, like Nerval, appears to have felt that more individualistic treatment of the tercets was permissible. Out of sixty-six sonnets with a regular octave, only twenty-nine have a regular sestet[7]. Of the remaining thirty-seven, twenty-one have a sestet of the *cdd cee* pattern. Since *A deux beaux yeux* falls into this main 'irregular' category, a detailed examination of its sestet will be of more than particular interest.

Unlike the disposition of rhyme in the regular sestet, which naturally coincides with a division into tercets, the irregular *cdd cee* pattern used so often by Gautier consists not of two tercets but of a quatrain and a couplet. However, in the poem in question, a further distinction presents itself: although the sestet may formally consist of a quatrain and a couplet, syntactically it reverts to a conventional division into tercets, each consisting of a completed tripartite sentence. The result of this is that l. 12 simultaneously belongs to the formal unity (ll. 9–12) of the quatrain *and* to the syntactical unity

of ll. 12–14, which, as we have seen, is also presented as a typographical unity. The effect of this is, on the one hand, to end the
poem on one of those satisfying couplets so often exploited by
English Renaissance sonneteers and on the other, to not too
heavily weight the last two lines of the poem in the way the Elizabethan couplet did. For whereas the *raison d'être* of the English
sonnet was the last couplet, this is certainly not the case with the
poem in question in which the climax is reached, as in the classical
French sonnet, in the first line of the second tercet. Now, in this
particular poem, everything conspires to focus attention on l. 12:
the conventional French typographical spacing is allowed to over-
ride the pressing formal demands of the quatrain, the ensuing
space between ll. 11 and 12 creating a pause for the taking of
breath before the pronouncement of the key line and at the same
time increasing the tension, since the reader awaits in suspense
the regaining of formal balance in which the rhyme of l. 9 is at last
confirmed by l. 12.

The fact that the couplet has still to follow l. 12 and bring the
poem to a close in no way detracts from that line's singular splen-
dour. For as sometimes was to be the case with Baudelaire, the role
of the final couplet was to be one of

> un écho, vague et perdu, de l'idée principale, une sorte de sonore cadence,
> de prolongement lumineux, de luxe inutile, "une dernière pirouette, une
> queue de comète," ajouta en souriant Mallarmé...[8].

Although, in Mallarmé's 'Elizabethan' sonnets, the final couplet is
far from being a 'luxe inutile', in those irregular hybrid sonnets first
developed by Gautier, in which a conventional French octave is
partnered by an English-looking sestet, Mallarmé's description of
the last couplet as a 'dernière pirouette' is not an inaccurate one.
And in the context of Baudelaire's *Correspondances* sonnet—to give
just one obvious example from that poet—it is no less appropriate
a definition:

> Il est des parfums frais comme des chairs d'enfants,
> Doux comme les hautbois, verts comme les prairies,
> —Et d'autres, corrompus, riches et triomphants,
>
> Ayant l'expansion des choses infinies,
> Comme l'ambre, le musc, le benjoin et l'encens,
> Qui chantent les transports de l'esprit et des sens.

The resemblance between the syntactical structure of Baudelaire's and Gautier's second tercet is striking:

> Ils sont si transparents qu'ils laissent voir votre âme,
> Comme une fleur céleste au calice idéal
> Que l'on apercevrait à travers un cristal.

Both follow a climactic l. 12 with a last long comparison that gently yet satisfyingly relaxes the tension that was built up in the earlier part of the sestet.

In the structure of its imagery the sestet of *A deux beaux yeux* is also original. Whereas in the octave the imagery was primarily concerned with expressing the radiance of the loved object's eyes, and the poet's task was that of scientifically observing without being hopelessly dazzled by them, in the sestet the poet's perceptive powers are better adjusted and more penetrating. In the octave it was only the object's qualities that were expressed—their jewel-like perfection, their 'vif rayonnement'—whilst in the sestet the poet is able to grasp their *significance*. The poet's material is the same in the sestet as it was in the octave but he works on it at a privileged remove: he not only sees but also understands.

Thus in l. 12, the poet, at the peak of his perceptive powers, sees the mirror-like opacity of the eyes magically clear to become transparent, a sheet of glass through which the poet perceives the very soul of the loved one:

> Ils sont si transparents qu'ils laissent voir votre âme.

In the final couplet, the 'âme', echoing the narcissistic imagery of ll. 9 and 10, undergoes a final, almost Mallarmean transformation and appears to the poet as a celestial flower through eyes that have taken on the spiritual and prophetic quality of crystal.

In the context of the 1830s, the importance and suggestiveness of Gautier's exploitation of the sonnet form in this poem is considerable: it is quite different from that of a Musset or a Sainte-Beuve. Perhaps the most effective way to emphasize Gautier's originality is to sketch Baudelaire's possible debt not only to the imagery of *A deux beaux yeux* but also to its structure. For a poem like *Sed non satiata,* with its suggestive movement from an exotic and lyrical octave to an ironically perceptive sestet, and its relatively banal but in this case highly significant use of the rhymes 'âme' and 'flamme', has a forerunner in Gautier. Similarly, Baudelaire's

Le Flambeau vivant may derive inspiration from Gautier since four of its rhyme words — 'âme' and 'flamme' (again), 'beau' and 'flambeau' — and much of its imagery comes from *A deux beaux yeux*. And Baudelairian sonnets as different as *Correspondances, Les Chats, Tristesses de la lune* and *Que diras-tu ce soir* . . . may to a greater or lesser degree owe either formal inspiration or imagery to this early poem.

Although this sonnet shows Gautier to be already in the 1830s aware of the sonnet's potential, he did curiously little, between 1845 and 1865, to develop the form further. *Emaux et camées* (1852), Gautier's 'recueil capital' according to René Jasinski[9], contains only one sonnet and apart from the *Sept Sonnets à Marie Mattéi*, contemporary with *Emaux et camées* but to be found in *Dernières Poésies*[10], the 1845–1865 period seems to have been a relatively sterile one for Gautier the sonneteer. Perhaps this was because Gautier felt that the octosyllabic line, which dominates in *Emaux et camées*, did not lend itself particularly well to the sonnet, most of Gautier's sonnets being in alexandrines, although he did write a few in octosyllables and decasyllables. Nevertheless, Gautier's theoretical enthusiasm for the sonnet is continued throughout this period, as the following extract from his review of Evariste Boulay-Paty's *Sonnets de la vie humaine* (1851) seems to confirm and in terms which support the kind of sonnet practice we have noted in his own sonnets of the 1830s:

> Le sonnet nous vient d'Italie, ce pays du rythme arrêté, de la forme précise, où il y a trop de soleil pour que l'on souffle le vague et le brouillard dans la pensée ou dans l'expression. Ce vase étroit, taillé à facettes, transparent et pur comme le cristal, ne peut admettre qu'une goutte d'essence : topaze, diamant ou rubis pour la couleur ; ambre, myrrhe ou cinname pour le parfum. Pétrarque y mit ses larmes sur les rigueurs de Laure, et y enferma ses soupirs. La précieuse liqueur, l'odeur suave ne sont pas encore evaporées du flacon fragile, mais bien fermé. . .[11]

Boulay-Paty (1804–1864) was himself the author of an octosyllabic sonnet on the sonnet called *Pipée* in which, curiously enough, given the bird/sonnet analogy he develops, he evades the *sonnet/sansonnet* rhyme used, as we shall see, both by the seventeenth-century sonneteer Saint-Amant in his sonnet on the sonnet and by Nerval in his sonnet *Epitaphe*. Displaying none of the critical pretentions we shall observe in other sonnets on the sonnet, Boulay-

Paty's *Pipée* is a simple exercise in the picturesque:

> J'aime en rimeur, presque en amant,
> Les sonnets, dont la troupe ailée
> S'ébat dans mon ciel, par volée,
> Avec un frais gazouillement.
>
> Appelant leur essaim charmant,
> Ma folâtre muse, isolée,
> Au fond de la forêt voilée
> Les pipe à moi bien doucement.
>
> Quand j'en tiens un, je le caresse
> Avec bonheur, avec tendresse.
> Je le sens longtemps palpiter,
>
> Puis, en lissant sa jeune plume,
> Je l'encage dans mon volume,
> Le beau sonnet, pour y chanter.

Gautier's sonnet on the sonnet was not written until 1870, at the end of a decade which had been a notably rich one for the sonnet whether written by Gautier himself or by other poets of *Le Parnasse contemporain* (including Mallarmé, Heredia and Verlaine as well as Baudelaire, Leconte de Lisle and Banville). In looking back and summing up sonnet developments so far, Gautier reflects however not so much the complex developments in the sonnet that, inspired perhaps by his own sonnets of the 1830s, had been elaborated by, for example, Baudelaire in the 1840s and 50s, as the more specifically Parnassian developments in the sonnet exemplified in the work of Leconte de Lisle, Banville and Heredia.

It is interesting to compare Gautier's theories in his sonnet on the sonnet of 1870 with those of Théodore de Banville (1823–1891) who expresses his ideas on the sonnet at about the same time in his *Petit traité de poésie française* of 1872. Not surprisingly, the two theories share many similarities and both reflect what is a fundamentally 'Parnassian' attitude to the sonnet form. Banville was, of course, like Gautier, a highly competent sonneteer. His first efforts in this form appear in *Les Cariatides* (1842) and some of his later sonnets reveal a preoccupation with rhyme which is often openly expressed. In a sonnet of 1875, for example, dedicated to Gabriel Marc, in which he takes care to fit both the words 'Gabriel' and 'Marc' into the rhyme-scheme, Banville declares:

> La rime est tout, mon cher cousin GABRIEL MARC!

...
C'est pourquoi soignons bien nos rimes, GABRIEL.[12]

but it was in his *Petit traité* that Banville gave fuller expression to his theory of rhyme and also of the sonnet:

> La forme du Sonnet est magnifique, prodigieusement belle, — et cependant infirme en quelque sorte; car les tercets, qui à eux deux forment six vers, étant d'une part *physiquement* plus courts que les quatrains, qui à eux deux forment huit vers, — et d'autre part *semblant* infiniment plus courts que les quatrains, — à cause de ce qu'il y a d'allègre et de rapide dans le tercet et de pompeux et lent dans le quatrain; — le Sonnet ressemble à une figure dont le buste serait trop long et dont les jambes seraient trop grêles et trop courtes.[13]

Meanwhile, Gautier, in his sonnet on the sonnet *(Poésies complètes*, III, p. 204), has this to say:

> Les quatrains du Sonnet sont de bons chevaliers
> Crêtés de lambrequins, plastronnés d'armoiries,
> Marchant à pas égaux le long des galeries
> Ou veillant, lance au poing, droits contre les piliers.
>
> Mais une dame attend au bas des escaliers;
> Sous son capuchon brun, comme dans les féeries,
> On voit confusément luire des pierreries;
> Ils la vont recevoir, graves et réguliers.
>
> Pages de satin blanc, à la housse bouffante,
> Les tercets, plus légers, la prennent à leur tour
> Et jusqu'aux pieds du Roi conduisent cette infante.
>
> Là, relevant son voile, apparaît triomphante
> La *Belle*, la *Diva*, digne qu'avec amour
> Claudius, sur l'émail, en trace le contour.

The correspondence between these two theories of the sonnet is remarkably close. Banville describes the quatrains as 'lents' and 'pompeux' and in Gautier's poem they become personified as 'bons chevaliers':

> Crêtés de lambrequins, plastronnés d'armoiries,
> Marchant à pas égaux...

Meanwhile, Banville's theoretical recognition of the tercets' 'légèreté' and 'rapidité' coincides with Gautier's definition of them:

> Pages de satin blanc, à la housse bouffante,
> Les tercets, plus légers...

Although this stress on the agility and flexibility of the sestet is very pertinent since its three pairs of rhymes give it far more variety than the regular octave's quadruple repetition of the same two rhymes, the concept of 'légèreté' is nonetheless ambiguous. For, looked at from the point of view of Gautier's earlier sonnet *A deux beaux yeux* (and from the point of view of a sonneteer like Baudelaire, as we shall presently see) the essential movement of the sonnet seems to be one not from heaviness to frailty but from expansiveness to concentration. As Z. L. Zaleski, in a theoretical article on the sonnet, affirms:

> Les strophes du sonnet semblent osciller aussi entre la sévérité compacte des quatrains et la densité dynamique des tercets . . .[14]

It is the sestet then that is the most powerful and dynamic part of the poem, the main theatre of action, in which the poet comes into closest contact with his material, concentrating and purifying it. In the following chapter on the Symbolist sonneteers, Baudelaire's use of the sonnet will bear this remark out with particular clarity.

Gautier is right, on the other hand, to reserve the unveiling of the poem's essential message—personified in his sonnet as the lady *incognito*—for the end of the sestet in which she appears in her most brilliant and suggestive form as the *'Diva'*. Similarly, Banville correctly stresses the revelatory value of the tercets when he affirms:

> Ce qu'il y a de vraiment surprenant dans le Sonnet, c'est que le même travail doit être fait deux fois, d'abord dans les quatrains, ensuite dans les tercets,—et que cependant les tercets doivent non pas répéter les quatrains mais les éclairer, comme une herse qu'on allume montre dans un décor de théâtre un effet qu'on n'y avait pas vu auparavant.[15]

The dramatic potential of the sonnet sestet that Banville recognizes here was one that Baudelaire was not only to exploit himself but also to recognize in the Lyonnais sonneteer Joséphin Soulary (1815–1891) to whom he wrote in 1860:

> Vous dramatisez le sonnet et vous lui donnez un dénouement[16].

Baudelaire perhaps overrated Soulary as a sonneteer (unlike Barbey d'Aurevilly and J. Lemaître who criticize the author of the *Sonnets humoristiques* (1858) sharply[17]) but Soulary was nevertheless an agile *metteur en scène* within the sonnet's strict limits and, if often largely inconsequential, his sonnets seldom lack vitality and even wit—as we see in his sonnet on the sonnet (from the *Sonnets humoristiques*), in which the poet slips deftly into the corsets and bodices of a restricting form:

Je n'entrerai pas là, —dit la folle en riant,—
Je vais faire éclater cette robe trop juste!
Puis elle enfle son sein, tord sa hanche robuste,
Et prête à contre-sens un bras luxuriant.

J'aime ces doux combats, et je suis patient.
Dans l'étroit vêtement, vrai corset de Procuste,
Là, serrant un atour, ici le déliant,
J'ai fait passer enfin tête, épaules et buste.

Avec art maintenant dessinons sous ces plis
La forme bondissante et les contours polis.
Voyez! la robe flotte, et la beauté s'accuse.

Est-elle bien ou mal en ces simples dehors?
Rien de moins dans le cœur, rien de plus sur le corps,
Ainsi me plaît la femme, ainsi je veux la Muse.

But what does the Parnassian theory of the sonnet add up to and was it made good by its exponents in practice? In the first place, the stress on the importance of rhyme in the sonnet seems after 1840, and particularly thanks to Gautier, to have been increasingly accepted, to the extent that the sonneteer often openly acknowledged that rhyme was his *point de départ*. As well as Gautier's *bouts rimés* and Banville's sonnets stressing the primacy of rhyme, the following only half-completed sonnet of Heredia (1842–1905) offers an interesting illustration of the compositional priorities of the mid-century sonneteer:

L'Autodafé

Riff
serge
vierge
juif

suif
verge
cierge
vif

Cet homme seul debout blond à la grosse lippe
Grave et blême, vêtu de noir, c'est Don Philippe
Le peuple le regarde avec un vague effroi

Et quand la chair prend feu sous l'huile qui l'arrose,
Il croit voir s'animer le visage du roi
Au joyeux flamboiement de l'Autodafé rose.[18]

As well as illustrating the prime importance of rhyme, this sonnet also shows, as Gautier and Banville had also seemed to suggest, that the sestet was seen, on the whole, to be the more fundamental part of the sonnet—to the extent that it could be composed *before* the quatrains which preceded it. A minor Breton poet, Auguste Brizeux (1803–1858), carried this idea to its logical conclusion in devising a sonnet in which the tercets were *followed* by the quatrains:

Les rimeurs ont posé le sonnet sur la pointe,
Le sonnet qui s'aiguise et finit en tercet:
Au solide quatrain la part faible est mal jointe.

Je voudrais commencer par où l'on finissait.
Tercet svelte, élancé dans ta grâce idéale,
Parais donc le premier, forme pyramidale!

Au-dessous les quatrains, graves, majestueux,
Liés par le ciment de la rime jumelle,
Fièrement assoiront leur base solennelle,
Leur socle de granit, leurs degrés somptueux.

Ainsi le monument s'élève harmonieux,
Plus de base effrayante à l'œil et qui chancelle,
La base est large et sûre et l'aiguille étincelle,
La pyramide aura sa pointe dans les cieux.[19]

Although the terms in which Brizeux describes the sonnet's quatrains and tercets anticipate those of Gautier and Banville quite strikingly, this poem is perhaps less interesting in itself than the possible influence it had on later and greater French sonneteers of the century —for example, Baudelaire in *Bien loin d'ici*, Verlaine in *Résignation* (to mention but one of Verlaine's reversed sonnets) and Corbière in *Le Crapaud*, all of these latter three poets exploiting the sonnet in this inverted form one way or another.

Both Brizeux and Soulary had also sometimes composed sonnets in which the conventional order of the sonnet's quatrains and tercets was rearranged. Soulary for example, experiments with the sonnet's form quite effectively in his *La Rencontre (En train express)* in which the rhythm of the enclosed tercets accelerates as the express trains rocket past each other, slowing down only in the final quatrain when the passing train has disappeared:

Tel on voit l'éclair croiser un éclair,
Le train lancé frôle un train sur la voie.
Ne dirait-on pas deux oiseaux de proie
En sens opposés se disputant l'air?

N'est-ce pas Wilhelm emportant Lénore?
Si prompt qu'ait filé l'ardent météore,
En croupe après lui mon cœur s'est lancé.

Ah! c'est qu'au passage une lèvre fraîche
M'a sournoisement décoché la flèche
D'un sourire aigu dont je suis blessé!
Folle vision! cruelle est ma joie!
Car, dans ce sourire entré sous ma chair,
Ce n'est pas l'espoir, ô fantôme cher,
C'est l'adieu fatal que ta bouche envoie!

Baudelaire, again, was later to use this technique, though to different effect, in his curious sonnet *L'Avertisseur*.

These latter examples must not however give the impression that the Parnassian sonneteers—Gautier, Banville, Leconte de Lisle, Heredia—were deeply experimental in their use of the sonnet, for this was not the case. Soulary and Brizeux, both provincial poets, were only on the margins of the Parisian Parnassianism of the 1850s and 60s[20] and complement, or take to extremes, rather than exemplify Parnassian tendencies of this period. For although they experimented with rhyme words, rare and exotic combinations of rhyme constantly being sought, the chief Parnassian poets were largely content with the sonnet structure as it was, as it had been inherited by them from the sixteenth and seventeenth centuries. As Heredia remarked, according to Henri Potez:

Le sonnet est une poème lyrique d'une forme déterminée.
Il faut en avoir le sens mathématique et mystique.[21]

and he goes on to make an implicit criticism of Baudelaire's experiments with the sonnet form:

Les sonnets de Baudelaire sont de beaux poèmes: ils ont leur charme propre, qui est exquis, mais ce ne sont pas des sonnets.[22]

For the Parnassian sonneteers therefore, apart from Gautier and Banville, there seemed little point in theoretical discussion. Their aims were exemplified above all in practice and are illustrated perhaps at their best in the regular perfection of Heredia's *Les Trophées* (1893) in which typical Parnassian themes—mythological and historical figures, objects and events—become converted within the sonnet's chiselled and mathematical framework, into a series of fixed and memorable marmoreal images.

III

THE SYMBOLIST SONNET

(i) *Nerval*

Although a contemporary of Gautier, Nerval (1808–1855) was not a 'Parnassian' poet. Although, like Gautier and his younger contemporaries—Leconte de Lisle (1818–1894) and Banville (1823–1891)—Nerval recognized the decorative potential of the sonnet form, with its elegant profile and intricate rhyme-scheme, he did not exploit it, as the Parnassians sometimes seemed to, for its own sake. Nerval will not, for example, use the sonnet's chiselled framework to fix a marmoreal image or summarise an historical or mythological event as Heredia does in *Les Trophées,* nor will he use it to give epigrammatic point to a moral argument or an eloquent address as Leconte de Lisle does in sonnets like *Aux morts, Fiat nox* and *Aux modernes (Poèmes barbares,* 1862–1872).

For Nerval, the sonnet's function was not so much to narrate or describe—even with the utmost precision and objectivity— a known truth or established event as itself to discover fresh knowledge, new truths; its function was not merely to supply a fitting framework for something already established but was itself to establish something; it was not to content itself with chiselling and polishing, as the Parnassians tended to, the already static and solidly established block of Carrara marble but to capture and fuse the many volatile and sometimes seemingly incompatible molecules of a far more fluid and mercurial substance. But why was it that Nerval's subject matter should be this 'mercurial substance' rather than the

Vers, marbre, onyx, émail

of Gautier and the Parnassians?

Basically, the answer is that Nerval's subject matter was, as it rarely was for the Parnassians, his *own* personality. For the twelve sonnets of *Les Chimères* reflect in a way quite unprecedented in the nineteenth-century French sonnet, an attempt to resolve (using the same qualities of precision and objectivity that the Parnassians had bestowed on other themes) the tensions and complexities of the poet's personality and experience. In making this attempt, Nerval is of course rehabilitating to a certain extent a function of the sonnet that had been understood and exploited by the great sonneteers of the Pléiade. Like the Du Bellay of *Les Regrets,* for example, the Nerval of *Les Chimères* was attempting to relate himself to the changing landscapes—native (French), foreign (Italian) and mythological (Greek)—of his experience and to the fleeting objects of his aspirations and desires (the loved woman or the divine or archetypal image). Far more than Sainte-Beuve thus, Nerval reconnected the nineteenth-century French sonnet to its fertile sixteenth-century roots and in doing so helped it to flourish in his own poetry with renewed freshness and vigour.

But did Nerval develop a theory of the sonnet? The much neglected sonnet *Epitaphe* does not claim to represent a coherent sonnet theory nor is it in any real sense a 'sonnet on the sonnet' but it nevertheless exemplifies many of the fundamental tendencies and characteristics of the Nervalian sonnet. Besides, any sonnet which rhymes on the word 'sonnet' invites careful examination since it inevitably becomes in a sense a sonnet talking about itself. Of course, Nerval's sonnet rhyming on 'sonnet' was not without precedent; the prolific seventeenth-century sonneteer Saint-Amant, in his deliberately foreshortened 13-line sonnet, will assert:

> Là faisant quelquefois le pas du Sansonnet,
> Et dandinant du cu comme un sonneur de cloche,
> Je m'esgueule de rire, escrivant d'une broche
> En mots de Pathelin ce grotesque Sonnet.[1]

whilst in the sixteenth-century Molinet's *Art de rhétorique* the following list of rhyming words and phrases is to be found:

> sansonnet   (l'oiseau)
> sans son net
> sans sonnet   (le poème)
> sans son est   (il est sans son)[2]

However, if, as these examples suggest, the 'sonnet'/'sansonnet' rhyme is a relative commonplace (for the sixteenth and seventeenth if not for the nineteenth century), this in no way detracts from the potential interest of Nerval's sonnet. For the poet who asks Death to wait until

> . . . il eût posé le point à son dernier sonnet

evokes, on the one hand, exactly the kind of image, both ludicrous and poignant, that poets of the 'Ironic Line', as we shall see in

Chapter Four, will be so successful in creating (compare, for instance; the last line of Laforgue's *Apothéose)* and, on the other, stresses, and this on a serious level, the urgency of the poet in his attempt to come to terms with his personality and experience in view of creating an epitaph valid both for himself and for posterity:

> Il a vécu tantôt gai comme un sansonnet,
> Tour à tour amoureux insoucieux et tendre,
> Tantôt sombre et rêveur comme un triste Clitandre,
> Un jour il entendit qu'à sa porte on sonnait.

> C'était la Mort! Alors il la pria d'attendre
> Qu'il eût posé le point à son dernier sonnet;
> Et puis sans s'émouvoir, il s'en alla s'étendre
> Au fond du coffre froid où son corps frissonait.

> Il était paresseux, à ce que dit l'histoire,
> Il laissait trop sécher l'encre dans l'écritoire.
> Il voulait tout savoir mais il n'a rien connu.

> Et quand vint le moment où, las de cette vie,
> Un soir d'hiver, enfin l'âme lui fut ravie,
> Il s'en alla disant: "Pourquoi suis-je venu?"

For Nerval, poetry was a kind of cognitive epitaph and this remark applies as much to the sonnet *Epitaphe* as to the sonnets of *Les Chimères* like *El Desdichado*. For in all his sonnets, Nerval is attempting, as we suggested, to relate and sum up the conflicting aspects of a life and personality and to resolve disparities between ambitions and achievements. But in what way was the sonnet a particularly suitable medium for achieving this ambition?

The recurrence throughout Nerval's sonnets of phrases like 'tantôt' and 'tour à tour'—as in line 13 of *El Desdichado:*

> Modulant tour à tour sur la lyre d'Orphée

and line 2 of *Epitaphe*

> Tour à tour amoureux insoucieux et tendre

(both of which refer to the structure of the poet's personality and actions)—is not without significance in the context of the sonnet's internal structure. For the sonnet is itself a kind of 'tour à tour' mechanism. Its two-rhyme octave (to which Nerval consistently has recourse though not always in its standard form) is, for example, a system of 'tour' and 'retour' in which two contrasting rhymes organize themselves into a system of complements and oppositions.

In *El Desdichado*, for example, the *same* rhyme sound is incorporated into words of *opposite* meaning:

Je suis le Ténébreux, —le Veuf, —l'Inconsolé

Dans la nuit du Tombeau, Toi qui m'as consolé

whilst in l. 7 the same rhyme sound ('désolé') heightens the implications of its first twin ('Inconsolé) whilst contradicting that of its second ('consolé').

Similarly, in the first quatrain of *Epitaphe*, the poet's alternating moods:

Il a vécu tantôt gai comme un sansonnet,
Tour à tour amoureux insoucieux et tendre,
Tantôt sombre et rêveur comme un triste Clitandre . . .

are also given expression by rhymes which, as in *El Desdichado*, harmonize in sound but not necessarily in sense. Thus the juxtaposition of 'tendre' with the inconsequential figure of 'Clitandre', expresses both the passionate and the playful side of the poet's personality. These contrasts become related, in the second quatrain, to more serious considerations, in this case the approach of Death; in this stanza, the cold and ominous rhyme 'frissonnait' contrasts with the lively and cheerful 'sansonnet' of 1. 1, the 'étendre' of 1. 7, not referring to the lover's bed anticipated by the 'tendre' of 1. 2 but to the 'coffre froid' of 1. 8.

Meanwhile, in the context of the sonnet's structure as a whole, the 'tours' of the quatrains are complemented by the 'retours' of the tercets in which the material of the octave is reconsidered and analysed under a different light. Thus in *El Desdichado*, the affirmations of the first line of the first quatrain:

Je suis le Ténébreux, —le Veuf, —l'Inconsolé

are subject to interrogation, to analysis in different terms in the first line of the sestet:

Suis-je Amour ou Phœbus? . . . Lusignan ou Biron?

In the sestet of *Epitaphe*, Nerval exploits the epigrammatic qualities of the sonnet to relate even more closely and economically the contrasts of the octave. Thus the general themes of ll. 9 and 11:

Il était paresseux, à ce que dit l'histoire

and

Il voulait tout savoir mais il n'a rien connu

become in ll. 10 and 14 more specifically related to those of the creative poet:

> Il laissait trop sécher l'encre dans l'écritoire
> Il s'en alla disant: "Pourquoi suis-je venu?"

Nerval was fully conscious of the dialectical structure that the sonnet provided for his thought and experience. In his preface to *Les Filles du feu,* addressed to Alexandre Dumas, he wrote, not without irony, of his sonnets:

> ils ne sont guère plus obscurs que la métaphysique de Hégel . . .[3].

For, as *El Desdichado* illustrates, Nerval's thought often develops in the manner of an Hegelian dialectic: the antitheses which are developed, half unconsciously, in the octave, become, in the sestet, consciously recognized and an attempt is made by the poet to bring them together and synthesize them. This synthesis of disparates, of the obsessive romantic images of melancholy and destruction with the classical images of light and order, is achieved on the imaginative level of the poem itself, the last tercet both completing the sonnet and resolving the tensions that were set up in the earlier stanzas:

> Et j'ai deux fois vainqueur traversé l'Achéron:
> Modulant tour à tour sur la lyre d'Orphée
> Les soupirs de la Sainte et les cris de la Fée[4].

The sonnet *Myrtho* also illustrates Nerval's attempt to resolve the apparently contradictory aspects of his aspirations and experience and express them as an aesthetic unity. For in this poem Nerval also endeavours to create through poetry an absolute union of the two sides of his personality, to promote a kind of mystic marriage of the poet and the Muse, of the contingent individual 'moi' of Nerval, and Myrtho, the symbol of his higher ambitions, the mythical idol to whom he aspires.

In doing this, Nerval takes into account (he could hardly fail to do so) the temporal events—loves, voyages, accidents which make up the fabric of his life, but these become significant to him (and to us) only when they are related to some archetypal gesture, figure or act that transcends them. The last line of the octave in *Myrtho* is particularly revelatory here:

> Car la Muse m'a fait l'un des fils de la Grèce.

For, in making Nerval a poet, the Muse has placed him in a mythological world, one inhabited by legendary figures with whom he is
bound to relate himself. In other words, in becoming a poet, Nerval
becomes increasingly sensitive to the values, gestures and acts of
a more ancient and permanent archetypal order. It is for this reason
that Nerval introduces religious, mythological or other archetypal
figures into his poetry. They represent the ideal roles, more tangibly
symbolized, that the Muse has delegated to him. In *Myrtho,* as
indeed in *El Desdichado,* it is to the role of poet that Nerval's personality most energetically aspires since it is through poetry, the
modern mythology, that he hopes to confer upon the accidents of
his experience an *absolute* significance. For Nerval then, poetry
itself is able to create the divine order that the chaos of reality
ordinarily lacks. For as he suggests in the last tercet of *Myrtho,*
it is under the auspices of poetry—'sous le laurier de Virgile'—that
is achieved the union of the contingent and the absolute, the delicate
hybrid hydrangeas of individual experience with the archetypal
exploits of mythological lore symbolized by the green myrtles:

> Toujours, sous les rameaux du laurier de Virgile,
> Le pâle hortensia s'unit au myrte vert!

If poetry is to provide for Nerval the solution in this way to
fundamental problems of existence it has to be submitted to the
most careful surveillance. The Romantic tendency to abandon willed
control to inspiration was one that had to be kept firmly in check.
Instead, a strict discipline was required to remind the poet always
to be conscious of his next move. It was here that the sonnet again
provided the poet with the ideal formal structure. On the one hand,
there was no room in it for unchecked lyricism or hyperbole, description or narration: there was none of the Romantic poem's
spaciousness into which eloquence could overflow. For the sonneteer is constantly obliged to keep his eye on the poem's always
rapidly approaching point of closure, to discipline his subject matter
in view of a conclusion that is always near at hand. On the other
hand, the highly conscious formal technique demanded by the
sonnet encouraged a similar degree of self-consciousness in the
poet's attitude towards his creative role.

One of the most important consequences of this self-consciousness and of this need for concentration, was Nerval's development

of the literary symbol as a means of expressing the essential facets of a complex idea or of his personality. As we saw, the sonnet imposes very severe limits on the scope of a poem's thematic developments. If Nerval is to obtain the same powerful effect as the long Romantic poem in a fraction of the space, his thought has to develop not only horizontally but also in depth. We have already noted how Nerval's thought tended to seek a point of synthesis at which the contrasts and antitheses of its various facets became united and resolved. In order to arrive at this point of synthesis and achieve this depth of significance, Nerval attached new importance to the poetic image or symbol. For the latter expresses the profound and yet complex thought of Nerval better than any other means. Its great advantage to him lies in its capacity to express both the unity and the wide-ranging suggestiveness of his ideas: it is the ideal form of poetic synthesis.

In the sonnet *Horus,* for example, Nerval attempts to create a cosmic drama through the mere juxtaposition of a few carefully chosen images. In this poem, 'Le dieu Kneph', the Egyptian God of Creation, is threatening chaos and destruction:

> C'est le dieu des volcans et le roi des hivers!

Against him is set the Goddess Isis, the universal Mother. The dramatic nature of this confrontation of powerful personalities is expressed in the very structure of the octave's images. The flashing green eyes of the Egyptian goddess in l. 5:

> Et l'ardeur d'autrefois brilla dans ses yeux verts

contrasts with the king's 'œil louche' of l. 7 whilst half the images in the rhyme position—'farouche', 'pervers', 'bouche', 'louche'—referring directly to Kneph—throw into dramatic relief the rage, corruption and decay that are the essence of his personality. The response of Isis, the opposite figure, is similarly intense in its theatricality:

> Isis, la mère, alors se leva sur sa couche,
> Fit un geste de haine à son époux farouche...

She then proceeds to address an imaginary audience in terms both ironic and dramatic:

> "Le voyez-vous, dit-elle, il meurt, ce vieux pervers,
> Tous les frimas du monde ont passé par sa bouche,

Attachez son pied tors, éteignez son œil louche,
C'est le dieu des volcans et le roi des hivers!"

Whereas it is the octave of *Horus* that sets the scene and states the conflict of the two leading characters, it is in the sestet that the action takes place and the *dénouement* resolves the tensions of the octave and expresses the action's moral or meaning. Thus the creation of a new universal order is reflected in the dramatic scene changes of the sestet in which Isis reappears dressed in Cybèle's robes before disappearing across the water on her golden conch, the heavens being triumphantly decked out with Iris's scarf. This latter image of the rainbow provides the perfect unifying symbol to the drama of the poem: it evokes the promise of a new order after the old chaos, symbolizing in Christian terms the fulfilment of God's promise to Noah after the flood, and in more general aesthetic terms expressing a mood of symmetry and serenity in which all the colours of experience are harmoniously united in a perfect arc. Summing up the poem in an image of intense visual as well as religious, mythological and moral suggestiveness, the rainbow represents the Nervalian image *par excellence,* one which confirms J.-P. Richard's comment that Nerval's

> vocation particulière est de rassembler dans l'espace d'une parole à la fois modeste et brillante une extraordinaire richesse d'idées, d'images, de sentiments.[5]

One of the great advantages of symbols of this sort is that they do not necessarily require an elaborate historical context. Nerval, with his tendency towards religious syncretism, will not hesitate, as we have just seen in *Horus,* to evoke a Christian symbol in pagan terms whilst in *El Desdichado* images have their source in many differing cultures or mythologies. Indeed, by losing the spacious narrative or descriptive context that it enjoyed in the long Romantic poem, the Nervalian image gains in prominence and autonomy. For in becoming isolated from its broader context, the image gains in versatility: it is more easily incorporated into an aesthetic pattern. The sonnet, by providing this aesthetic pattern, in many ways becomes the ideal context for it. We have already noted how in *El Desdichado, Epitaphe* and *Horus* the sonnet rhyme-scheme provided the perfect setting for contrasting and powerful images, and how, in *Myrtho* and *Horus,* the sonnet's last line encapsulated the poem's last great unifying symbol: in the first quatrain of *Horus,* it has been suggested[6] that Nerval even has recourse to acrostics (in English) to underline the poems two principal themes:

Le dieu Kneph en tremblant ébranlait l'univerS:
Isis, la mère, alors se leva sur sa couchE.
Fit un geste de haine à son époux farouchE,
Et l'ardeur d'autrefois brilla dans ses yeux vertS.

When Henri Lemaître suggests that the poetry of Gautier and his closest followers is largely:

fait avec des images—dont beaucoup *pourraient* devenir des symboles, ce qui explique qu'on trouve ici des pressentiments mallarméens ou valéryens: mais ces images restent des images, ou alors le poème devient un simple "object esthétique"[7]

he is making a distinction pertinent to any comparison between the Parnassian and the Nervalian sonnet. For Nerval (with Baudelaire, though in a different way) is the first 'Symbolist' sonneteer in that his sonnet's images are given a depth of suggestiveness, a range of potential reference that is on the whole lacking in the sonnets of Gautier, Leconte de Lisle and Heredia.

One of the side effects of this greater suggestiveness is the difficulty or 'obscurity' of Nerval's sonnets. Many attempts have recently been made to elucidate their complexity and to clarify their many potential levels of reference. The intention of this short section on Nerval has not been, however, so much to explore these aspects of the Nervalian imagination as to attempt to show why the sonnet was such a suitable form for expressing them. For, in *Les Chimères,* we do not see the sonnet exploited, as it was by the Parnassians, as an elegant and definitive structure for some largely descriptive or discursive development, but as a means of crystallising a destiny. Thus in the Nervalian sonnet, each rhyme word, each carefully isolated image, is an essential facet of the poet's personality, each of the poem's structural moves reflecting some profound tendency of his spiritual life. The very composition of a sonnet becomes thus for Nerval, as we saw in *Epitaphe* and in the sonnets of *Les Chimères,* the origin and context of a questioning of the poet's and the poem's essential roles and their relationship with the fundamental issues that life poses.

Introduction

Unlike Sainte-Beuve or Banville, Baudelaire did not adopt the sonnet form on the basis of a purely academic theory or for reasons of literary nostalgia. His sonnets are the work not of a virtuoso but of an artist for whom the selection of a particular form was never an arbitrary question. As Gide remarks:

> il n'est rien, chez Baudelaire, qui ne réponde à quelque interrogation de son esprit critique, à sa constante investigation, et c'est bien par cette conscience de lui-même et de son art qu'il s'élève au-dessus des vagues et faciles transports de ses plus éminents contemporains.[1]

The modernity of Baudelaire lies partly in his awareness of the paradoxes of experience. *Les Fleurs du Mal,* as the title suggests, give expression not so much to Ideas and Objects as to tensions and antitheses. The conflict between imaginative or spiritual aspirations on the one hand, and the need for contact with the real and physical on the other, is the central dilemma of the Baudelairian experience. To give adequate expression to these complexities, the poet requires a form capable of embodying the harmonies and tensions, the dualism of experience. The sonnet was to provide Baudelaire with just such a form.

It is easy to understand Baudelaire's antipathy for the 'facile transport'; it contradicted both his temperament and his artistic capabilities. In *Les Paradis artificiels* Baudelaire describes the experience of a certain hashish-eater:

> "J'étais", disait-il, "comme un cheval emporté et courant vers un abime, voulant s'arrêter, mais ne le pouvant pas. En effet, c'était un galop effroyable, et ma pensée, esclave de la circonstance, du milieu, de l'accident et de tout ce qui peut être impliqué dans le mot *hasard,* avait pris un tour purement et absolument rapsodique."[2]

This terror of the 'rhapsodic' experience may be closely related to Baudelaire's distrust of the 'facile transport', in which the lyric poet, 'esclave de la circonstance', abandons himself to the flux of inspiration. Baudelaire, as Barbey d'Aurevilly emphasized, was a 'Volontaire' rather than an 'Inspiré'[3]. The laws of his aesthetic universe were to be preordained, thus theoretically excluding any element of 'hasard'. For example, the limits of a poem, its end, became for him as important as its beginning. Like Poe,

un de ses axiomes favoris était encore celui-ci: "Tout dans un poëme comme dans un roman, dans un sonnet comme dans une nouvelle, doit concourir au dénouement."[4]

In praising the sonnet form's 'beauté pythagorique'[5], Baudelaire recognized its quality of almost mathematical exactitude. The sonnet was for him a poetic theorem that both expressed and defined a complex formula whose solution was often summed up in the last line with a mathematician's rigour and logic. As in a mathematical formula, the sonnet was an integral structure in which all parts were related to the whole. There was nothing superfluous or fortuitous about its symmetry. In *Mon cœur mis à nu* Baudelaire writes that:

> la régularité et . . . la symétrie . . . sont un des besoins primordiaux de l'esprit humain, au même degré que la complication et l'harmonie[6]

and in his poetry he will attempt, in aesthetic terms, to satisfy the same fundamental need. Thus the Baudelairian sonnet sometimes becomes the embodiment of the Intellect's struggle to grasp and express the potentially infinite flux of experience:

> Je ne vois qu'infini par toutes les fenêtres...
> . . .
> —Ah! ne jamais sortir des Nombres et des Etres!

Like the Pascalian mathematician of *Le Gouffre,* the sonneteer has an 'esprit de combinaison de d'analyse'[7]. His method of composition is one that attempts to balance equations or establish relationships between conflicting movements and disparate phenomena.

Just as Baudelaire was quick to recognize the intellectually satisfying qualities of the sonnet, he was also perhaps the first great nineteenth-century poet to exploit fully the suggestive potential of formal compression:

> Parce que la forme est contraignante, l'idée jaillit plus intense...Avez-vous observé qu'un morceau de ciel, aperçu par un soupirail ou entre deux cheminées, deux rochers, ou par une arcade, etc...., donnait une idée plus profonde de l'infini qu'un grand panorama vu du haut d'une montagne?[8] —

On the other hand, he is aware of the ornamental qualities of the sonnet's integrated but complicated framework:

> Comme un beau cadre ajoute à la peinture,
> Bien qu'elle soit d'un pinceau très-vanté,
> Je ne sais quoi d'étrange et d'enchanté
> En l'isolant de l'immense nature,

Ainsi bijoux, meubles, métaux, dorure,
S'adaptaient juste à sa rare beauté;
Rien n'offusquait sa parfaite clarté,
Et tout semblait lui servir de bordure.

Just as in *Le Cadre* the woman is defined to a significant degree by her setting, so the formal shape of the verse plays an essential part in the definition of the poem. In this way the sonnet is able to provide Baudelaire with a form capable of condensing both the vitality and the complexity of his experience into the profound unity which was his fundamental requirement of both art and life.

Octave and Sestet

> Ce que Baudelaire cherchait dans la forme, c'était la correspondance esthétique qui traduisit parfaitement sa donnée psychologique.[9]

The French sonnet tends, like Baudelaire, to have a split personality. For the division between octave and sestet, traceable, according to one theory[10], to the thirteenth-century origin of the sonnet as the union of the Italian *strambotto* and the Sicilian *sextine,* was always, outside England, a basic one: it marked the point at which the material of the poem underwent a major transformation. In the Baudelairian sonnet, this 'transformation' generally involves a marked shift in angle of perception, a revision of the poet's attitude towards his material that has far-reaching effects on the overall significance of the poem.

In the majority of Baudelaire's sonnets, whereas the octave tended to be discursive, the sestet was analytical or visionary. Its primary quality was its perceptiveness—its ability on the one hand to clarify or re-assess, often ironically, the preceding quatrains, and on the other to elaborate their implications and reveal their ultimate significance. Its function was, like the mind or spirit, to interpret and synthesize the raw experience, the sense data of the octave. Images of perception—'œil', 'yeux', 'prunelle'—and mental or spiritual apprehension—'âme', 'cerveau', 'esprit', 'cœur'—show a marked recurrence in the Baudelairian sestet. Indeed the words 'âme' and 'yeux' become its *leitmotiv*. Of course there are occasions when these words appear in the sonnet octave rather than in the sestet (and sometimes they appear in both) but the ratio of appearance of these 'key words' is about two to one in favour of the sestet. And this is no chance phenomenon since, as following examples will confirm, the key words tend to appear precisely at that pivotal point in the poem which marks the division of octave from sestet, that is, l. 9.

The line of demarcation between octave and sestet thus becomes the point at which the critical eyes of the tercets become turned towards the quatrains and, through them, the poet's mind or spirit sets about perceiving and analysing the significance of the octave's sensations. Although the eyes, because of their traditionally more penetrating quality, become, in the Baudelairian 'psychology' of the sonnet, the most privileged of the mind's sensory agents, the 'sense data' of the octave are not always transmitted to the sestet in visual terms. The sestet of *La Musique* expresses the *mental* analogy of the quatrain's music:

> l.9 Je sens vibrer *en moi* toutes les passions

whilst in *La Cloche fêlée,* the sestet is the spiritual replica of the octave's discordant sensations:

> l. 9 Moi, mon *âme* est fêlée . . .

In *La Fin de la journée,* the physical exhaustion and nervous irritability of the end of the day have, in the sestet, their spiritual analogy:

> ll. 9–11   Mon *esprit*, comme mes vertèbres,
> Invoque ardemment le repos;
> Le *cœur* plein de songes funèbres...

whilst in *Parfum exotique,* a complex of olfactory sensations is translated, in the sestet, into a pattern of spiritual nostalgia:

> ll. 12–14   . . . le parfum des verts tamariniers
> Se mêle dans mon *âme* au chant des mariniers.

The sestet of *Causerie* expresses the *emotional* resonance of the octave's disturbing images:

> l. 9 Mon *cœur* est un palais flétri par la cohue . . .

whilst the moral disquiet of *Le Mauvais Moine* is expressed in the sestet's images of spiritual decay:

> l. 9 Mon *âme* est un tombeau . . .

Within this broad range of moral and sensual reference however, analogies that link images of eyes and spirit are the most recurrent. There are many examples but the following are two of the most striking. In *Sed non satiata*, it is through the loved object's eyes that the poet is able to penetrate to her soul:

l. 9 Par ces deux grands yeux noirs, soupiraux de ton *âme* . . .

whilst in *Le Chat* the first line of the sestet marks the point at which the attributes of the cat become imaginatively identified with those of the woman:

l. 9 Je vois ma femme en *esprit* . . .[11]

A brief analysis of this latter sonnet will attempt to clarify in greater detail the nature and implications of the octave/sestet 'transformation' that we have just summarized. In *Le Chat* the function of the octave appears in many ways to be a kind of *preparation* for the symbol: it chooses an object, in this case a cat, and, at first, merely juxtaposes it with the poet's mood:

Viens mon beau chat, sur mon cœur amoureux

the word 'sur' here indicating a relationship of physical contact but not necessarily of metaphorical fusion. Indeed, throughout the octave, tendencies towards the latter—that is, the complete fusion of the physical object with the poet's mental state—are evaded with considerable subtlety. For already in l. 3 the poet's desire to gaze into the cat's eyes takes on a metaphorical potential:

Et laisse-moi plonger dans tes beaux yeux

which in l. 9 of the sonnet *Sed non satiata* is sufficient, as we have just seen, to plunge the poet into the spiritual register:

Par ces deux grands yeux noirs, soupiraux de ton âme . . .

Instead of this however, the metaphorical impetus of the third line of *Le Chat* is absorbed by the merely descriptive developments that close the proposition in the following line:

Mêlés de métal et d'agate.

A tendency to check lyrical enterprises in this way, aided by the alternating deca- and octosyllabic verse lines, is systematized in the octave. For the lyricism of each comparatively expansive deca-syllable:

Viens, mon beau chat, sur mon cœur amoureux
Et laisse-moi plonger dans tes beaux yeux
Lorsque mes doigts caressent à loisir
Et que ma main s'enivre du plaisir

is in turn absorbed into the more descriptive developments of the shorter octosyllabic lines:

> Retiens les griffes de ta patte
> Mêlés de métal et d'agate
> Ta tête et ton dos élastique
> De palper ton corps électrique.

Only after the second quatrain is sufficient lyrical impetus built up to sweep the poet into the metaphorical register as the lyricism of the octave overflows into the sestet:

> Lorsque mes doigts caressent à loisir
> Ta tête et ton dos élastique
> Et que ma main s'enivre du plaisir
> De palper ton corps électrique,
> Je vois ma femme en esprit . . .

This latter proposition, so carefully and yet only implicitly prepared in the octave, becomes analyzed and extended in the sestet. Whereas every one of the octave's procrastinations was the excuse to evoke a fresh sensual nuance (the octave as a whole representing a kind of symphony of tactile sensations ranging from the sharpness of the cat's claws to the elaborate variations in stroking and caressing of the second quatrain), in the sestet sensual evocations have a more complex purpose. Although the subject matter of each of the tercets—eyes and body respectively—is the same as that of the quatrains, it becomes subject to a more far-reaching or ironic form of analysis. For in the sestet it is not only the sensations of the body but the perceptions of the spirit that come fully into play. In describing the physical attributes of the woman, the poet reveals a more acute awareness of spiritual overtones: he not merely describes but interprets the objects before him. Thus the sensual qualities of the cat's eyes:

> Mêlés de métal et d'agate

are, when they become those of the woman, redefined in terms both sensual and figurative:

> Son regard,
> Profond et froid. . . .

Similarly, the sensual pleasure the cat's smooth coat affords the poet is nuanced, when the body becomes that of a woman, with mysterious and dangerous overtones that have their repercussions in the poet's emotional and spiritual as well as merely physical sphere:

> Et, des pieds jusques à la tête,
> Un air subtil, un dangereux parfum,
> Nagent autour de son corps brun.

Le Chat thus demonstrates how the sonnet provides Baudelaire with a structure that enables both his lyrical and sensual and his critical and intellectual faculties an even share of fulfilment. Metaphorical developments are not allowed too obtrusively or prematurely to interrupt spontaneous lyrical tendencies and yet, at the same time, these latter are not permitted, as was sometimes the case in the Romantic poem, to become indefinitely indulged. For the shift into the sestet, as we saw with Nerval, reminds the poet that the poem is already nearing its close and that it is time for the meaning or significance of the preceding eight lines' experience to be given unified expression. The sestet becomes thus a medium of interpretation and unification: it places in significant relation (very often as a metaphor) the objects which the octave merely describes or juxtaposes.

Jean Prévost suggests that Baudelaire was attracted to the sonnet

> comme l'une des formes les plus *concises* et les plus *immobiles* de poèmes, comme l'une des formes poétiques aussi où l'opposition des deux groupes de rimes et des deux mouvements—les tercets après les quatrains—peut servir une opposition ou un retournement de la pensée.[12]

This 'retournement', one that was to become an essential part of the Symbolist poet's creative process, is incorporated in the very structure of the sonnet form. For the relationship between the poet and the poem is mirrored in the relationship between the sestet and the octave, since the poet is obliged by the very form of the verse to look back critically at his own work, to gaze with objective lucidity at his own lyricism. And just as to do this he is obliged to distance himself from his verse, similarly, this distance is symbolically incorporated in the poem itself: it is visible in the spacing between octave and sestet that French poets (unlike their English counterparts) had tended to maintain. For the sestet does not merely follow the octave: it becomes in itself a kind of *criticism* of the octave in which the former's lyrical expansiveness and ratiocination are are reassessed from a critical distance. In this way the sestet becomes a kind of poem *about* the octave. A poem about a poem, a poet analyzing and criticizing a poet—these are of course essential themes of the Symbolist aesthetic and it is easy to see how well the sonnet form lends itself to their expression.

In Arsène Houssaye's sonnet *Les Quatre Saisons,* which appeared in the first volume of *Le Parnasse contemporain* in 1866, these latter tendencies become allegorized. The sonnet's point of departure is a direct enquiry as to its function:

—Sonnet, que me veux-tu?

This question is given an answer in the first quatrain which expresses the poet's initial lyrical impulses in a series of positive, primordial images:

—Je chante les saisons!
Le PRINTEMPS en sa fleur est l'amoureux poëte
Qui souffle dans les luths de la forêt muette,
Depuis les chênes verts jusqu'aux neigeux buissons.

In the second quatrain, the expansion of the poet's imagination is evoked in similarly Romantic terms:

L'ETE, c'est un penseur à tous les horizons:
Le matin il s'éveille aux chants de l'alouette,
On voit jusques au soir flotter sa silhouette . . .

In the sestet however, quite a different trend of development is established. The lyrical images of the octave's golden summer are not further expanded but broken down and analyzed into their constituent parts. An autumnal first tercet, for example, admirably illustrates the sudden and withering transformation of the octave's verdant imagery:

L'AUTOMNE est un critique effeuillant la ramure
Pour voir le tronc de l'arbre et rêver sous le houx . . .

whilst in the second tercet, the Romantic 'penseur à tous les horizons' is replaced by a far more critical and self-conscious poet. For the soul which, in the octave, the poet permitted to expand with the rising lark, now becomes as much an object for cool analysis as any of the other lyrical images:

L'HIVER, un misanthrope, un spectateur jaloux
Qui siffle avec fureur, dans l'ouragan qui brame,
Les roses, les épis, les raisins et son âme.

The sonnet's special ability in this way both to expand lyrically and at the same time to contract intellectually, to fuse the Romantic imagination with the critical intellect, made it the ideal medium for the poet living in the immediate wake of a post-Romantic reaction. For Baudelaire, for example, the sonnet fulfilled what were for him the 'deux qualités littéraires fondamentales: surnaturalisme et ironie.'[13] The Baudelairian sonnet is thus able to combine and relate the disparate perceptions of the mid-nineteenth-century mind with new effectiveness and integrity.

Sonnet Types

According to Banville[14], the only strictly regular French sonnet is the *abba abba ccd ede* form. In spite of his overwhelming preference for irregular patterns, Baudelaire wrote five of this type, some of which, surprisingly, figure amongst his best. *Sed non satiata,* for example, in many ways typifies the Baudelairian sonnet at its most accomplished, as it moves inwards from a lyrical celebration of a woman's physical beauty to an examination of her soul. In this poem, the parenthetic rhyme-scheme of the regular Petrarchan octave is given particularly rich development. For the magnificent paired rhymes—'havane', 'savane', 'pavane', 'caravane'—are like exotic fans which, when momentarily opened, flash their seductive messages before being closed again between their dark, parenthetic rhymes 'nuits', 'minuits', 'nuits', 'ennuis'.

As Cassagne has noted[15], Baudelaire could not have shown greater virtuosity in his use of 'rime riche' than he does in the octave of this poem. For he uses the only four rhymes in '-avane' that exist in the French language, whereas if he had contented himself with the 'rime suffisante' '-ane', he would have had 160 words at his disposal.

In the sestet of *Sed non satiata,* the shift into the spiritual sphere is achieved. The tercets, like the two dark eyes which they evoke, are the 'soupiraux' through which the lover penetrates to the underworld of the 'sorcière d'ébène' 's soul, with its black imagery of Proserpine and the Styx. The crucial appearance of the word 'âme' in the first line of the sestet once again brings with it a readjustment of the poet's attitude towards his material: the lyrical exultation of the octave is contrasted with the morbid irony of the sestet with its negative assertions:

l. 11 Je ne suis pas le Styx . . .

l. 12 Hélas! et je ne puis . . .

and its lucid awareness of the lack of spiritual foundation for the physical and emotional promise of the quatrains:

l. 10 O démon sans pitié . . .

The 'bizarre déité' becomes a 'Mégère libertine' and the ecstacy anticipated in the 'elixir de ta bouche' is realized not in an African paradise but in a Pagan hell.

Baudelaire also uses a Petrarchan octave configuration in some of his irregular sonnets. In *Correspondances*, for example, the parenthetic rhyme-scheme manoeuvres the most important substantives of the poem—'paroles' and 'symboles', 'unité' and 'clarté', with their supernatural dazzle—between rhymes of enclosure and familiarity—'piliers' and 'familiers', 'confondent' and 'répondent'. The choice of four rhymes here instead of the normal two, is not due to a lack of verbal inventiveness: it is deliberate. For the four enclosed substantives that they constitute are the essential concepts of the sonnet's metaphysical theme. To have restricted the rhyme-scheme to two rhymes would have seriously impaired the balanced disposition of the argument. As it is, Baudelaire is able to create the perfect compromise: he maintains the essential parenthetic structure of the Petrarchan octave but introduces four rather than two rhymes, creating thus a greater effect of contrast and variety within unity than would otherwise have been possible. In this way he is able to remain faithful both to his subject matter and to his choice of form.

The desire to shock, not through vulgarity but through a deliberate and often 'savant' refusal to observe given forms, that is as deeply entrenched in Baudelaire's code of behaviour as in his aesthetic ideas, has further repercussions in his sonnets. For the irregular pattern of many of them is neither a chance phenomenon nor a sign of Baudelaire's technical incompetence. On the contrary, Baudelaire's concept of irregularity is backed up by an aesthetic theory:

ce qui n'est pas légèrement difforme a l'air insensible;—d'où il suit que l'irrégularité, c'est-à-dire l'inattendu, la surprise, l'étonnement sont une partie essentielle et la caractéristique de la beauté[16].

This equation of 'irrégularité' and 'beauté' takes on a deeper significance in the context of Baudelaire's later experiments with the sonnet form, notably in *L'Avertisseur* and in the reversed sonnet *Bien loin d'ici*. For interference with the formal structure of the Baudelairian sonnet has repercussions in the thematic development of the poem. *Bien loin d'ici* opens with a pair of tercets in which, through a series of clear demonstrative assertions, an Ingresque woman is described reclining luxuriously on cushions. After the statement

l. 7 C'est la chambre de Dorothée

however, the next seven lines, instead of commenting in a new way on the preceding material, merely elaborate on it in a vague and expansive manner until the poem is brought to a close on the quiet catastrophe of the last line:

—Des fleurs se pâment dans un coin.

In a letter to Catulle Mendès of 29th March 1866, Baudelaire took pains to stress the vagueness and distraction that characterized this line:

Le dernier vers de la pièce . . . doit être précédé d'un tiret (—), pour lui donner une forme d'isolement, de distraction.[17]

For this inversion of the conventional sonnet pattern causes the more typical thematic movement of the Baudelairian sonnet to be similarly reversed. Sensations, in the sestet, tend to be blurred and distant:

l. 8 —La brise et l'eau chantent au loin . . .

and instead of moving inwards to the clarity and concentration of the mind or spirit, consciousness slowly but progressively expands until finally, reaching a point of dissolution, it melts into unconsciousness—as in a swoon.

In *L'Avertisseur* the sonnet form is given even more bizarre treatment, since in this poem the tercets are enclosed between two leisurely but aphoristic quatrains:

Tout homme digne de ce nom
A dans le cœur un Serpent jaune,
Installé comme sur un trône,
Qui, s'il dit: "Je veux" répond "Non!"

Plonge tes yeux dans les yeux fixes
Des Satyresses ou des Nixes,
La Dent dit: "Pense à ton devoir!"

Fais des enfants, plante des arbres,
Polis de vers, sculpte des marbres,
La Dent dit: "Vivras-tu ce soir?"
Quoi qu'il ébauche ou qu'il espère,
L'homme ne vit pas un moment
Sans subir l'avertissement
De l'insupportable Vipère.

Baudelaire's intention here seems to have been, echoing thematic tendencies, to inject the negative venom of the tercets into the very heart of the poem.

Conclusion

More than any other great poet of the century Baudelaire was aware of the potential richness and variety of the sonnet form. As he suggests in a letter to Armand Fraisse of the 18th February 1860:

Tout va bien au Sonnet, la bouffonnerie, la galanterie, la passion, la rêverie, la méditation philosophique.[18]

On the one hand, the Baudelairian sonnet constitutes a genuine renewal of the French and Italian sonnet traditions[19] in which the old themes are given real rejuvenation, not merely the academic or casual airing with which Sainte-Beuve and Musset had been content. *Epigraphe pour un Livre condamné, Le Flambeau vivant, 'Que diras-tu ce soir...', Duellum* and *Le Coucher du soleil romantique* respectively represent nineteenth-century versions of old sonnet types—the epigram, the enigma, the 'galanterie', the 'passion' and the polemic. On the other hand, Baudelaire supplements the traditional categories with newer, more complex themes—the 'méditation philosophique' of sonnets like *Correspondances, Obsession* and *Le Gouffre,* or the 'rêverie' of *Parfum exotique* or *Recueillement*—that were profoundly to influence the Symbolist tradition.

A glance at the first volume of *Le Parnasse contemporain* (1866) immediately reveals the effect, in some cases profound, that the Baudelairian sonnet had on the sonneteers of the next generation.[20] One of the fundamental tendencies of Baudelaire's sonnets was, as we saw, to move away from the relatively straightforward lyrical, descriptive or even didactic style, effected by Romantic sonneteers like Sainte-Beuve or Parnassians like Leconte de Lisle, to a different mode of development. The octave/sestet change of register was of central importance in this since the shift from quatrains to tercets usually, as we saw, coincided with a shift into a new and more concentrated sphere of poetic significance. In this latter, language's function increasingly became no longer that, as it was still for the Parnassians, of describing objects or events but of evoking complex and suggestive mental states. Images that were for Gautier and Banville on the whole largely decorative became, in Baudelaire's sestets, increasingly metaphorical.

Now it is above all the manner in which this shift in tone from octave to sestet is achieved that betrays Baudelaire's influence on his immediate successors whose work was beginning to appear in the first volume of *Le Parnasse contemporain*. In Eugène Lefébure's *Le Pingouin,* for example, we see a kind of abortive (because launched rather late in the poem—see l. 11) attempt to give the purely descriptive developments of the first half of the poem a symbolic dimension:

> Allongeant dans l'air vide un regard hébété,
> Les pingouins sont groupés aux pointes des presqu'îles,
> Et la mer saute autour de ces spectres tranquilles,
> Immobiles témoins de sa mobilité.
>
> On ne les verra pas s'élancer dans l'orage,
> Car leurs pauvres moignons ne peuvent voltiger,
> Le ciel les déshérite, et, s'ils veulent nager,
> L'Océan dédaigneux les rejette au rivage.
>
> D'une imbécilité calme que rien n'émeut,
> Ils se laissent en cercle assommer sur la grève . . .
> Et moi, je sais un être abruti qui ne peut
>
> Nager dans l'action ou planer dans le rêve,
> Fixe, les bras pendants, les yeux perdus au loin,
> Ah! l'assomera-t-on bientôt, ce vieux Pingouin?

Here, not only is the mechanism of the metaphor strongly reminiscent of Baudelaire but also the terms in which it is couched: l. 12, for example, is clearly derived from *Les Fleurs du Mal*.

In the same volume of *Le Parnasse contemporain,* the sestet of Heredia's *La Conque* also shows signs of Baudelairian influence. For after a lyrical and reflective octave:

> Oh! qui dira jamais, conque fine et nacrée,
> Dans combien d'océans, pendant combien d'hivers,
> Tu supportas, au choc enflammé des éclairs,
> L'assaut tumultueux de la haute marée!

Maintenant, sous le ciel, parmi les fucus verts,
Tu t'es fait un doux lit dans l'arène dorée.
Mais ton espoir est vain. Longue et désespérée,
En toi pleure à jamais la voix sombre des mers . . .

the sestet effects the shift from the descriptive to the metaphorical that converts the conch into a symbol of the poet's soul:

Mon âme est devenue une prison sonore.
Et comme dans ton sein roule et soupire encore
Un regret affaibli de la grande clameur;
Ainsi, du plus profond de ce cœur. . .

The second tercet however betrays Heredia's lack of expertise in conducting sustained metaphorical enterprises since suddenly, in l. 12, the thematically quite unanticipated and subsequently unexplained apparition of 'Elle' attempts (but does not succeed because left too late and completely unsubstantiated) to give a more precise emotional direction to the sestet:

Ainsi, du plus profond de ce cœur trop plein d'Elle,
Triste, lente, insensible, et pourtant éternelle,
Toujours monte une étrange et confuse rumeur.

Here, Heredia does not closely relate the female figure to the central theme of the poem, give it flesh and blood and a distinctive aura or perfume as Baudelaire does in sonnets like *Sed non satiata* or *Le Flambeau vivant*. Because of this, 'Elle' remains a colourless and uninspiring abstract presenting no suggestive detail onto which the reader's imagination can latch. It is perhaps because of his insecurity in the metaphorical or symbolic register that Heredia gave up the Baudelairian approach to the sonnet and reverted to the largely descriptive mode of the Parnassians. As Pierre Martino confirms:

La poésie de Heredia n'est point du tout symbolique: sur cent-vingt sonnets, trois—et ce sont les premiers en date—affectent la forme du symbole.[21]

Nothing could be less true of Mallarmé whose sonnet *Le Sonneur*, which also appeared in the 1866 volume of *Le Parnasse contemporain*, impeccably recreates the thematic structure and tone of Baudelaire's sonnets like *La Cloche fêlée*. Unlike any other of Baudelaire's imitators so far mentioned, Mallarmé gives the metaphorical relationship established between 'moi' and 'le sonneur', in the first line of the sestet, real coherence, makes of it an emotional and moral reality. Whereas for Heredia in *La Conque* it was enough merely to pronounce the magic formula 'Elle' to explain why his soul should be compared to a conch, for Mallarmé, the 'moi'/ 'sonneur' analogy is more thoroughly developed: it is not merely picturesque but highly symbolic. For the contemplation of the 'sonneur' hearing the distant notes of his bells absorbed into the heavens *becomes* the poet struggling with a recalcitrant medium to find an ideal means of expression:

> Je suis cet homme. Hélas! de la nuit désireuse,
> J'ai beau tirer le câble à sonner l'idéal,
> De froids Péchés s'ébat un plumage féal,
>
> Et la voix ne me vient que par bribes et creuse!

As these new developments in the sonnet of the 1860s therefore show, it was Baudelaire who was to become the chief source of inspiration for a fresh attitude towards poetry, one that was to direct it towards the exploration of some of the central problems of poetic creation—the nature and value of metaphor and symbol as means of poetic communication and the relationship between the poem's formal and thematic developments—that were to remain, and indeed still remain for twentieth-century poets, issues of fundamental importance. The function of the following section on Mallarmé will partly be to elucidate these issues and to show how Mallarmé's exploitation of the sonnet, perhaps more than any other of his poems, reveals an insight into the profound workings of poetry that surpasses even that of Baudelaire.

(iii) *Mallarmé*

The Mallarmean sonnet, unlike that of Baudelaire, is not fundamentally the expression of an aesthetic transformation of experience. It finds its inspiration not so much in the physical and sensory stimuli of reality as in the virtualities of language itself:

> Ainsi le chœur des romances
> A la lèvre vole-t-il
> Exclus-en si tu commences
> Le réel parce que vil.... *(Toute l'âme résumée)*

In Mallarmé's later and most characteristic sonnets[1], the creative process is not one that moves from experience through language to art, but from language to art and thence experience. Unlike the best

Baudelairian sonnets in which the tensions between 'forme' and 'fond' are perfectly balanced, the 'fond' of the Mallarmean sonnet is always the function of the 'forme'. It is language itself, not a prior experience, that provides the revelation. Words will not servilely copy an arbitrary and always ambiguous reality but, on the contrary, oblige reality to mould itself around them. Thus language and not experience becomes the poet's point of departure. Similarly, the intrinsic virtues of the sonnet form itself, rather than subject matter, become the chief source of poetic inspiration.

For Mallarmé, thus, the poet's function was not so much to describe an object or experience as more specifically to recreate its *beauty:*

> *Peindre, non la chose, mais l'effet qu'elle produit.*[2]

This 'effet' or beauty was one that was to be *verbally* recreated since beauty, for Mallarmé, is incarnated, not as it was for the Parnassians, in the object itself, but in that invisible and intangible halo that surrounds the object, bathing it in a suggestive light, which only the imagination perceives and which, for the poet, only language can express:

> A quoi bon la merveille de transposer un fait de nature en sa presque disparition vibratoire selon le jeu de la parole, cependant; si ce n'est pour qu'en émane, sans la gêne d'un proche ou concret rappel, la notion pure.[3]

The reversal of procedure implied here, in which the 'proche ou concret rappel' is discarded in favour of the 'notion pure', in which the Word is presented with the minimum of reference to a prior experience, and in which Beauty is recreated without its causes or origins in the poet's sensations being fully revealed, naturally demanded a similar reversal or alteration of compositional priorities. Now the sonnet was a form that provided for this exceptionally well. For in sonnet writing, very often, the rhyme-scheme and rhyme words were established *before* the logical phrase into which they would eventually become set. Hence, in part, the attraction of the sonnet to Mallarmé. For as Heredia's half-completed sonnet *L'Autodafé* illustrated, the sonneteer's point of departure was sometimes as much a rhyme-scheme as an experience, an emotion or an object. Rhyme, as Banville asserted in the *Petit traité de poésie française* (1872), was the source of beauty, the primary effect of poetry and he goes on to say that *'l'imagination de la Rime* est, entre toutes, la qualité qui constitue le poëte.'[4] In Mallarmé's mature method of sonnet composition it was similarly rhyme, the 'effect', that was established before its 'causes'. These latter were worked out later and as discreetly and ambiguously as possible: they lie concealed in the mysterious involutions of Mallarmean syntax which it is the role of the reader to unravel.

This complex process is illustrated in Mallarmé's *Sonnet en −yx,* composed, in its first form, in 1868, although it was not published until 1887 when it appeared in the *Poësies* as one of the great metaphysical quartet of sonnets called *Plusieurs sonnets.* An analysis of this poem here would be of interest for several reasons. Firstly, because it was perhaps the first truly *Mallarmean* sonnet, showing little trace of the Baudelairian influence so easily discernible in its predecessors of the first half of the decade. Secondly, it was the product of a very deliberate and conscious attempt, on Mallarmé's part, to explore the *sonnetness* of the sonnet, to investigate this poetic form's profound tendencies: the *Sonnet en −yx* becomes thus in every sense a sonnet on the sonnet, a *Sonnet allégorique de lui-même* as Mallarmé was himself to call it at the time of its original conception. And thirdly, this poem illustrates how the sonnet form will adapt itself to the reversal or complication of compositional priorities to which Mallarmé was increasingly to commit himself in his poetry after the 1860s. To simplify the discussion, we will quote here only the later (1887) version of this sonnet:

> Ses purs ongles très haut dédiant leur onyx
> L'Angoisse, ce minuit, soutient, lampadophore,
> Maint rêve vespéral brûlé par le Phénix
> Que ne recueille pas de cinéraire amphore
>
> Sur les crédences, au salon vide: nul ptyx,
> Aboli bibelot d'inanité sonore,
> (Car le Maître est allé puiser des pleurs au Styx
> Avec se seul objet dont le Néant s'honore).
>
> Mais proche la croisée au nord vacante, un or
> Agonise selon peut-être le décor
> Des licornes ruant du feu contre une nixe,
>
> Elle, défunte nue en le miroir, encor
> Que, dans l'oubli fermé par le cadre, se fixe
> De scintillations sitôt le septuor.[5]

In what way does this sonnet illustrate a reversal of compositional priorities? Mallarmé provides a clue to this problem when he remarks in a letter to Cazalis:

> J'extrais ce sonnet, auquel j'avais une fois songé cet été, d'une étude projetée sur *la Parole:* il est inverse, je veux dire que le sens, s'il en a un (mais je me consolerais du contraire grâce à la dose de poésie qu'il renferme, ce me semble) est évoqué par un mirage interne des mots mêmes. En se laissant aller à le murmurer plusieurs fois, on éprouve une sensation assez cabalistique.[6]

The sonneteer's aim becomes thus the production of 'un mirage interne des mots mêmes'; but what words will provide the basis of this mirage effect whilst, at the same time, strengthening, even defining, the form the poem will take? The answer to this question is of course the rhyme words and it will be the rhyme-scheme that becomes the poet's *point de départ*. As H. A. Grubbs affirms in his study of this poem:

> the sonnet, instead of being constructed from the inside (starting with a theme and finding rimes to give it form) was constructed from the outside (the rimes were found first and they created the theme).[7]

If the rhyme-scheme is to play this primary role in the poem it is obviously important that it should be original. The Parnassian predilection for *rime rare* is shared here by Mallarmé (though for different reasons) and in this sonnet Mallarmè chooses one of the most original and difficult rhyme-schemes possible. Sonneteers before Mallarmé had of course exploited difficult rhymes in '-ixe'; Baudelaire, for example, in the first tercet of the curious sonnet *L'Avertisseur* had rhymed 'fixes' and 'Nixes' whilst Banville had used the rhymes 'onyx'/'phénix', 'essor'/'d'or' in the sestet of the first sonnet in *Les Cariatides* (1842). No poet before Mallarmé had however attempted to apply these difficult rhymes not only in the sestet of a sonnet but also in the octave. Thus in Mallarmé's sonnet, not only did the octave require four rhymes in '-yx' and '-ore' but also, in the sestet, the same rhymes were taken up again with their gender reversed as '-ixe' and '-or'. The use of 'rimes croisées' rather than 'rimes embrassées' in the octave (unusual, after the 1860s, for Mallarmé who, except in his Elizabethan sonnets, prefers the enclosed rhymes of the regular French octave) is particularly interesting; for the alternating rhymes, like adjacent but contrasting facets of a polygon, exemplify the prismatic quality of a form in which words 's'allument de reflets réciproques comme une virtuelle traînée de feux sur des pierreries'[8] and thus create the right phonetic structure for the desired 'mirage interne des mots mêmes' that Mallarmé was seeking.

Of course, Mallarmé's choice of a supremely difficult rhyme-scheme presented him with special problems: were there, for example, enough words in '-yx' in the language to supply the octave rhyme-scheme? Mallarmé wrote in a letter to Lefébure of 3 May 1868:

> je n'ai que trois rimes in *ix*, concertez-vous pour m'envoyer le sens réel du mot ptyx: on m'assure qu'il n'existe dans aucune langue, ce que je préférerais de beaucoup à fin de me donner le charme de le créer par la magie de la rime.'[9]

In spite of the ironic tone, Mallarmé is also serious here for the presence of the three rhyme words 'onyx', 'Phénix' and 'Styx' legitimately demanded the existence of a phonetically matching fourth word to complete the poem's formal structure. Thus the imaginary word 'ptyx' is brought in as a cornerstone to the second quatrain.

Space in this short study unfortunately does not permit us to further the discussion that has since centred on this sonorous monosyllable but we cannot pass on to the other aspects of this sonnet that we want to treat here without remarking that Mallarmé's choice of the word 'ptyx' is a perfect illustration of the reversal of conventional compositional priorities that this sonnet exemplifies. For to choose (or even invent) a word for its sonorous qualities and only afterwards create a meaning or significance for it, was a strictly logical move for a sonneteer who had established his rhyme-scheme and was seeking to make some kind of sense of the 'mirage interne des mots' to which he had committed himself. Thus, in the second quatrain of this sonnet, the word 'ptyx', after (and only *after*) it has fulfilled its function as a rhyme receives, in the next line, the possibility of a meaning or even an ironic definition:

nul ptyx,
Aboli bibelot d'inanité sonore . . .

But to turn to our second point, in what sense is *Ses purs ongles* . . . a sonnet on the sonnet? In the following passage, Mallarmé draws our attention to three fundamental aspects of his creative method or intentions and suggests that this sonnet embodies them with particular effectiveness:

> Par exemple, une fenêtre nocturne ouverte, les deux volets attachés; une chambre avec personne dedans malgré l'air stable que présentent les volets attachés, et dans une nuit faite d'absence et d'interrogation, sans meubles, sinon l'ébauche plausible de vagues consoles, un cadre belliqueux et agonisant, de miroir appendu au fond, avec sa réflexion stellaire et incompréhensible, de la Grande Ourse, qui relie au ciel seul ce logis abandonné du monde.
>
> J'ai pris ce sujet d'un sonnet nul et se réfléchissant de toutes les façons, parce que mon œuvre est si bien préparé et hierarchisé, représentant comme il le peut l'Univers, que je n'aurais su, sans endommager quelqu'une de mes impressions étagées, rien en enlever, —et aucun sonnet ne s'y rencontre.[10]

The first of these three aspects—the idea of reflection—plays an essential role in Mallarmé's notion of poetic creation and leads him to seek out a form that will satisfy this demand. The sonnet as a form capable of 'se réfléchissant de toutes les façons' has much to recommend it. The sonnet octave for example consists of two separated quatrains whose self-reflecting rhymes provide a mirror image of each other. As Aragon suggests:

> il est de convention que les quatrains y soient comme les deux miroirs d'une même image ou miroir l'un de l'autre . . . une sorte de dilemme dans lequel le poète est enfermé[11].

But not only do the two quatrains reflect each other since the whole octave becomes in turn reflected in the sestet—a mirror that deliberately creates a measure of distortion. In the *Sonnet en –yx* Mallarmé emphasizes this point by using the same rhyme sounds in the sestet as in the octave except that he reverses the gender, thus creating the effect of a kind of inverted mirror image.

But why did Mallarmé require a form capable of reproducing various levels—phonetic, stanzaic—of interreflection? This question leads us directly to Mallarmé's second creative intention—that of the preparation and hierarchisation of his work. Mallarmé's concern with 'preparation' is reflected in his almost obsessive preoccupation with the idea of a *cadre*—a word that appears both in the *Sonnet en –yx* and in the passage describing it cited above. For the sonneteer, as we saw, the creation of a *cadre* was very often the *point de départ* of poetic composition: it took the form of a rhyme-scheme that was prepared *before* the internal constituents of the poem could be definitively arranged. We have already noted what Baudelaire suggested in his sonnet *Le Cadre:*

Comme un beau cadre ajoute à la peinture . . .

and with Mallarmé the aesthetics of the *cadre* are worked out even more thoroughly. Thus the sonnet octave supplies for Mallarmé a kind of window-framework, in this case 'une fenêtre ouverte, les deux volets attachés' opening to present or reveal the octave's subject: 'une chambre avec personne dedans . . . une nuit faite d'absence et d'interrogation . . .' When in the sestet, the *cadre* is no longer a window but a mirror frame—'un cadre belliqueux et agonisant, de miroir appendu au fond . . .', there is a corresponding change in the poem's formal 'cadre'. Unlike the balanced rhymes of the octave, the sestet *cadre* is more baroque: it embodies the curves and contorsions of a gilt mirror-frame, its golden rhymes in '-or' (four out of six) set off by the roccoco figure of the 'nixe'.

But with the framework prepared, the poet has to organize his 'impressions étagées' into a hierarchy and one of a significant or absolute order since, fulfilling his third creative intention, the poem was to represent the universe, 'représentant comme elle peut l'Univers'. Thus the *Sonnet en –yx,* and in this it sets the pattern for Mallarmé's great metaphysical sonnets of the 1880s to which it was to become closely linked, is a poem about the universe, or rather about the struggle of a consciousness to come to terms with the Unknown. It is in the ordering of the successive levels of this struggle that the sonnet really fulfils its role. For whereas the octave provides a window through which the despairing consciousness stares at the meaningless void of reality, the sestet provides an imaginative register in which the doubts of the octave (reality) become mirrored by the mind (the sestet) and take on a purer significance and form.

The sonnet becomes thus for Mallarmé the compact vision of a consciousness in which the author, having (as in the second quatrain) in allegorical terms announced his absence, leaves the stage free for the drama of the poem's creation. For the poem is the pure form that alone will reflect and, at the same time transcend, through its beauty, the inanity of reality, Instead thus of taking, as a Romantic poet might have done, his own experience as a point of departure for the drama, Mallarmé deliberately chooses the recalcitrant and objectively fixed framework of the sonnet: for by discarding the contingent experience or the accidental object, Mallarmé is able to direct his appeal along more profound and absolute, which means, for him, aesthetic, lines. It is not therefore the *décor* of 'Nuit' or the 'Angoisse' of experience but the 'scintillation' of Beauty that Mallarmé wishes to impress most firmly on the reader's mind. As Mallarmé asserted in a letter to Cazalis not long before this sonnet's composition—and here he is expressing what is for him a philosophical as well as emotional truth—

> Il n'y a que la Beauté—et elle n'a qu'une expression parfaite, la Poésie. Tout le reste est mensonge . . .[12]

In becoming thus an allegory of poetic creation, the *Sonnet en –yx* also becomes a *Sonnet allégorique de lui-même* for every important factor in the poem's composition—choice of rhyme-scheme, organization of phonetic and stanzaic patterns, hierarchical ordering of 'theme'—coincides with an essential aspect of the sonnet structure. By drawing attention to itself in this narcissistic manner therefore, the *Sonnet en –yx* draws attention to the complexity and beauty of the sonnet form and, in doing so, makes it much easier for us to understand how Mallarmé was able to draw such deep inspiration from it.

The compositional priorities that the *Sonnet en –yx* and Mallarmé's comments on it illustrate, become systematized in the great sonnets that follow—particularly in the 1880s and 90s. Since in the sonnet, it was rhyme more than any other feature that defined the form of the poem, by strengthening and enriching his rhymes, the poet strengthened and enriched the *form* of his verse. Because Form was for Mallarmé an absolute priority, in his sonnets rhyme will tend to take precedence over other considerations—such as syntax, for example.

In order to preserve the rhyme-word in its infrangible position, to maintain the purity of the form, logical and grammatical elements sometimes have to undergo profound modification. The anfractuosities of ellipsis and anacoluthon, inversion and parataxis, become in the Mallarmean sonnet a necessary accompaniment to formal perfection. Note for example in the first line of the sonnet *Eventail de Mme. Mallarmé*, the unusual crowding of prepositions before the rhyme word 'langage':

Avec comme pour langage. . . .

The complexity of the Mallarmean sentence also of course has its origins in the poet's temperamental predilection for the labyrinthine syntactical structures that are the basis of his prose style. J. Schérer affirms that:

> Si Mallarmé fait de l'inversion un usage systématique très étendu, c'est parce qu'un mot changé de place surprend, se remarque davantage, et acquiert une valeur nouvelle.[13]

The sonnet form's demands therefore confirm Mallarmé's own innate predisposition since, for him, it was by rearranging language's structure that its beauties and expressive possibilities become freshly apparent. Thus in the heptasyllabic *Marchande d'herbes aromatiques*, the syntactical inversions of the ninth and tenth lines create a phonetic situation which invites l. 12 to rhyme richly on the proper name:

> ll. 9–12   Mieux entre une envahissante
> Chevelure ici mets-la
> Que le brin salubre y sente,
> Zéphirine, Paméla . . .

Since the difficulties involved in re-arranging the word order of a phrase in order for it to fit into the compass of the line becomes intensified in sonnets of a shorter verse line (as in the above example) Mallarmé will increasingly cultivate sonnets of this sort. Nearly half Mallarmé's sonnets are in hepta- or octosyllables.

At the beginning of his poetic career, Mallarmé wrote to Cazalis:

> Tu riras peut-être de ma manie de sonnets . . . mais pour moi c'est un grand poème en petit : les quatrains et les tercets me semblent des chants entiers, et je passe parfois trois jours à en équilibrer d'avance les parties, pour que le tout soit harmonieux et s'approche du beau.[14]

and Mallarmé's comments here already reveal an awareness of the sonnet form's qualities that will profoundly affect his use of the sonnet. For the Mallarmean sonnet is a 'grand poème en petit': compressed within the strict boundaries of a fixed form, its language becomes concentrated and refined; images brought together as facets of a unified structure, set up a pattern of virtually infinite inter-reflection which in a mere fourteen lines will often provide the breadth of conceptual development more normally associated with the 'grand poème'. Meanwhile, the sonnet's separate stanzas—

the quatrains and the tercets—become 'des chants entiers' and enjoy a degree of autonomy which, permitting dramatic juxtaposition of different moods or reactions to experience, will enable complex themes to be developed on various, sometimes hierarchical, levels. Finally, the symmetry of the sonnet's structure, the harmonious balancing of its various parts, and the interaction of its intricate rhyme-scheme, will assure the ultimate Harmony and Beauty that for Mallarmé was achieved—beyond the nullity of reality and the anguish of emotional experience—only through Poetry.

IV

THE IRONIC LINE

(i) *Verlaine*

In an article on his contemporary Heredia—and in terms reminiscent, only without the irony, of his sonnet *A la louange de Laure et de Pétrarque* (1883)—Verlaine affirms:

> Cette forme suprême qui avait su gagner jusqu'au suffrage de l'à bon droit très difficile Boileau, que Pétrarque avait fondée sur du diamant, où Shakspeare [sic] fit rugir et sourire en divines magies la plus énorme de toutes les passions, et dont les Renaissants furent les bons marchands pour jusqu'à la postérité la plus reculée, le Sonnet, déjà triomphant à nouveau depuis 1830, eut en cet Espagnol superbement Français son grand poète définitif.[1]

When Verlaine himself writes sonnets however it is seldom in the manner of Heredia. On the contrary, his sympathies as a sonneteer lie rather with a poet like Musset who, earlier in the same article, he affirms:

> par le droit du génie, sinon chronologiquement, fut le véritable restaurateur du Sonnet en France[2].

For unlike Sainte-Beuve and Gautier who almost invariably adhered to the regular sonnet and who 'le réduisirent aux règles strictes', Musset 'le fit large, à sa main, pour ainsi parler . . .'[3].

These latter comments give considerable insight into Verlaine's attitude towards the sonnet for, after the Parnassian influence of the early 1860s had worn off, his primary demand of a poetic form increasingly seems to become that of *flexibility*—whether in terms of rhyme, rhythm or stanzaic form[4]. Verlaine wanted the sonnet to be for him, as it had been for Musset, a malleable instrument, adaptable to various moods or needs. In view of this it is not surprising to find that Verlaine's attitude towards the sonnet is changeable and ambiguous.

In the first place, the structure of the sonnet with its contrasting rhymes and the sestet's tendency towards analysis of the octave, was one that demanded, perhaps, too much organization of a *logical* nature to appeal consistently to Verlaine. His attempts to minimise the contrasts of the octave—as in *Nevermore,* in which, instead of alternating masculine and feminine rhymes in the conventional manner, Verlaine makes a suite of four masculine rhymes follow a suite of four feminine ones giving rise to a unity and monotony of tone quite unlike the variety and contrast of the conventional Petrarchan octave[5]—or to blur the line of demarcation between octave and sestet—as in *Une grande dame*—illustrate his attempt to replace a structure of contrasts and analyses by a simple lyrical statement.

Sometimes of course Verlaine does succeed, even within the strict confines of the regular sonnet, in creating this sort of purely lyrical development. In *Mon Rêve familier* for example, a regular octave, in a leisurely and expansive fashion, evokes the vague and yet penetrating apparition of the 'rêve' in veiled terms whilst in the sestet, any attempt to define and thus destroy the spectral beauty is warded off with Mallarmean expertise. Indeed, this sonnet is a miracle of finesse and restraint in which through a structure of subtle and persuasive rhythms:

> Et qui n'est, chaque fois, ni tout à fait la même
> Ni tout à fait une autre . . .

and seductive rhymes ('exila', 'elle a'), a fragile but absorbing mood or experience is evoked. Unfortunately, however, few of Verlaine's other 200-odd sonnets approach this standard. One reason for this is that the composition of mood poetry—at which Verlaine was at his most original and best[6]—was one that only occasionally succeeded within the rigid and complex structure of the sonnet. Although the sonnet octave's quadruple repetition of the same rhyme and the form's overall compactness and unity of tone were often able to help to create the desired monotony of effect (as in *Lassitude* whose first line

> De la douceur, de la douceur, de la douceur!

is re-echoed by the other octave rhyme words—'la sœur', 'berceur', 'obsesseur'), the scope for repetition of rhyme and unity of mood is extended in Verlaine's most characteristic works—the mood poems in *Eaux-fortes*, *Paysages tristes* and *Fêtes galantes* and *Romances sans paroles*—far beyond the formal rules operating in the regular sonnet. In *Soleils couchants,* for example, instead of being obliged to follow an octave on two rhymes with a sestet on three as he would in a regular sonnet, Verlaine enhances the monotony and symmetry of his mood by following with a second octave on two rhymes that furthermore picks up internally the 'chant' rhymes of the first octave. Similarly, *Crépuscule du soir mystique* is a kind of thirteen-line sonnet in which a two-rhyme octave is followed not by a sestet introducing two or three new rhymes but by a quintet continuing to rhyme on the *same* sounds as the octave.

Verlaine was thus not temperamentally suited to the sonnet in the way that Baudelaire and Mallarmé were and it is for this reason that almost from the start an ironic attitude towards the sonnet reveals itself in his poems. Already this becomes apparent in Verlaine's first major collection of verse—the *Poèmes saturniens* (1866).

Although at the time of the *Poèmes saturniens,* as its *Prologue* suggests, the influence of Parnassian poetic theory is considerable, Verlaine's attitude towards it is already complex. He exploits the imaginative potential of 'rime rare' but, like those of Gautier in the 1860s, his rhymes are often so esoteric as to become parodies of it. Rhymes like 'Velléda' and 'réséda' in *Après trois ans* or 'enfant' and 'olifant' in *Lassitude* are as Parnassian in character as many of those in Heredia's *Trophées,* but in the first tercet of *Résignation* there is already more than a trace of burlesque:

> Tout enfant, j'allais rêvant Ko-Hinnor,
> Somptuosité persane et papale,
> Héliogabale et Sardanapale!

In other Verlainian sonnets from the *Poèmes saturniens,* both the thematic and the formal traditions are subjected to parody. *A une femme* parodies the Petrarchan theme of the idealization of the woman. Anticipating the playful excesses in certain of the *Fêtes galantes*—for example, *Dans la grotte*—the lover's lament in this sonnet becomes increasingly shrill and hyperbolic until by the first tercet it has become ludicrous:

> A vous ces vers de par la grâce consolante
> De vos grands yeux où rit et pleure un rêve doux,
> De par votre âme pure et toute bonne, à vous
> Ces vers du fond de ma détresse violente.
>
> C'est qu'hélas! le hideux cauchemar qui me hante
> N'a pas de trêve et va furieux, fou, jaloux,
> Se multipliant comme un cortège de loups
> Et se pendant après mon sort qu'il ensanglante!
>
> Oh! je souffre, je souffre affreusement, si bien
> Que le gémissement premier du premier homme
> Chassé d'Eden n'est qu'une églogue au prix du mien!

In *Une grande dame,* Verlaine goes further: he parodies not only the theme of the *femme fatale* (the 'Ninon', 'non' rhymes reminiscent of those in Musset's *Sonnet au lecteur* in *Poésies nouvelles)* :

> Ses yeux froids où l'émail sertit le bleu de Prusse
> Ont l'éclat insolent et dur du diamant,
> Pour la splendeur du sein, pour le rayonnement
> De la peau, nulle reine ou courtisane, fût-ce
>
> Cléopâtre la lynce ou la chatte Ninon,
> N'égale sa beauté patricienne, non!

and

> Il faut—pas de milieu!—l'adorer à genoux,
> Plat, n'ayant d'astre aux cieux que ses lourds cheveux roux . . .

but also the literary technique of the sonneteer, particularly his ingenuity in searching for rhymes. The rhymes 'russe', 'Prusse', 'fût-ce', for example, are progressively daring in setting and theme, the last of the three, an *enjambement,* overriding the octave/sestet boundary and continuing the hyperbole of the octave into the sestet.

The sonnet following *Une grande dame* in *Caprices, Monsieur Prudhomme,* is in a different way ironic. For in this poem, the banality of the subject matter contrasts with the ingenuity of the style in which the rhymes 'les a' and 'coryza', 'maroufles' and 'pantoufles' are simultaneously ludicrous and accomplished:

> Quant aux faiseurs de vers, ces vauriens, ces maroufles,
> Ces fainéants barbus, mal peignés, il les a
> Plus en horreur que son éternel coryza,
> Et le printemps en fleur brille sur ses pantoufles.

Whereas Verlaine's critics[7] generally affirm that the *Fêtes galantes* (1869) and the *Romances sans paroles* (1874) are a logical development of the most original themes and tendencies of *Poèmes saturniens* (1866), this is not the case with the poetry of *Sagesse* (1881). For the poems in this collection, written after Verlaine's reconversion to Catholicism and his renunciation of the Bohemian life he had been living with Rimbaud, mark a fundamental change in his attitude towards poetry and one that did not necessarily have its causes and origins in his earlier creative efforts. The change is one that comes from without and therefore cuts across the lines of Verlaine's previous poetic development. Eléonore Zimmermann suggests that after *Sagesse:*

La volonté de trouver une expression nouvelle survit encore en Verlaine mais elle ne traduit plus de préoccupation vitale. La vérité existe désormais pour lui en dehors du poème et il n'a pas besoin de la créer par son art. La poésie n'est plus le seul moyen de dompter le chaos du monde.'8

Whereas for Mallarmé, as we saw, the sonnet was an effective means of imposing significant order on the arbitrary phenomena of the universe, for the Verlaine of *Sagesse* it had no such absolute powers. As E. Zimmermann rightly affirms, in the context of the believer struggling with his concept of the Divine, 'un cadre strict sauvera le poète du danger de balbutier incompréhensiblement en cherchant à rendre un élan ineffable'9 but the sonnet does not, for Verlaine, in itself provide the revelation. It was something external to poetry that did this. Poetry's function became thus a subordinate one: not that of imaginatively recreating reality but that of simply transcribing, neatly and eloquently, a predetermined conviction. Poetry was thus for Verlaine, after *Sagesse,* no longer, as it was for Mallarmé at this time, a revelation of Truth at its very source, but merely a means of describing and expressing a truth apprehended *without* the poem.

The first of Verlaine's cycle of ten holy sonnets, for example, presents no fresh revelation to the reader. The poem merely ex-expresses an established religious truth of which certain significant details are thrown into special relief by the form of the verse. The *enjambement* of l. 3, for example, converts an already expressive gesture into one even more pathetic:

Et mes pieds offensés que Madelaine baigne
De larmes . . .

In the sestet, phrases like 'comme c'était écrit' and the purely rhetorical nature of the questions of which it consists, further emphasize the established nature of the knowledge that is the subject matter of the poem:

Ne t'ai-je pas aimé jusqu'à la mort moi-même,
O mon frère en mon père, O mon fils en l'Esprit.
Et n'ai-je pas souffert, comme c'était écrit?
N'ai-je pas sangloté ton angoisse suprême
Et n'ai-je pas sué la sueur de tes nuits,
Lamentable ami qui me cherches où je suis?

Here, Verlaine's attitude becomes once more that of some of the French Romantics: subject matter, not form, is the absolute, the latter merely becoming the vehicle of the former.

When poetry's subject matter becomes pre-eminent in this way, its form will inevitably suffer a loss of prestige. The poet will no longer be prepared to devote his best energies to formal preoccupations and fixed forms—like the sonnet—will no longer command absolute respect. After *Sagesse* therefore, Verlaine's attitude towards the sonnet, with his attitude towards poetry, changes. Whereas, as we saw, in *Poèmes saturniens*, the sonnet form had been exploited with a nuance of irony, it was now accepted either completely and almost naïvely or even more overtly parodied. For when in a sonnet dedicated to the sonneteer Albert Mérat Verlaine writes:

> Nous étant dépouillés de tout banal émoi,
> Vivions dans un dandysme épris des seules Rimes

we accept him no more completely than we do in the very next poem of *Jadis et naguère—Art poétique*—in which he asserts the opposite:

> O qui dira les torts de la Rime?

The sonnets of *Jadis et naguère* (1885) and *Parallèlement* (1889), roughly divide themselves thus into two categories: conventional and burlesque. Verlaine's 'conventional' sonnets of this period, such as *Le Pitre, Intérieur, Pierrot, Le Squelette, Circonspection, L'Auberge, A Horatio, Le Clown, Luxures* or *Le Sonnet de l'homme au sable*, bear a remarkable resemblance to the Romantic sonnet at its worst. Ruth Moser notes in the context of Verlaine what we have already noted of a Romantic sonneteer like Sainte-Beuve:

> le sonnet, tel qu'il le manie, ne correspond plus en rien à la rigidité de la forme classique, à sa cohérence interne et externe. C'est tout juste encore une pièce de poésie qui s'arrête après quatorze vers.[10]

The last tercet of *Le Pitre*, for example, instead of providing some new or interesting insight into the subject matter of the octave, merely rounds off a prosaic anecdote in a prosaic manner:

> Mais ce qu'il sied à tous d'admirer, c'est surtout
> Cette perruque d'où se dresse sur la tête,
> Preste, une queue avec un papillon au bout . . . .

whilst few nineteenth-century French sonnets are as dreary and inconsequential as *Le Sonnet de l'homme au sable* and *Le Squelette*, laboured and uninspired excursions into the comic-macabre that compare unfavourably with the far more amusing and accomplished

Monsieur Prudhomme of the *Poèmes saturniens*. *Le Clown* and *Intérieur*, though perfectly regular, are but poor pastiches of Baudelaire, whilst in *L'Auberge* Verlaine uses the sonnet as an occasional descriptive piece in the worst manner of Wordsworth or Sainte-Beuve.

On the other hand, Verlaine's playful and ironic attitude towards the sonnet at this time *(Sonnet boiteux, A la louange de Laure et de Pétrarque, Ecrit sur l'album de Mme. N. de V., Vers pour être calomnié)* is a little more successful. These are the poems of a more relaxed Verlaine, their tone being reminiscent of the *Poèmes saturniens*. They are not however always as subtle as the latter. For in them, Verlaine is sometimes merely chipping at the surface of the sonnet, not subjecting it to any profound or perceptive interrogation. The ambiguous stylistic situations he creates appear sometimes to be without any real point or resolution: the intention of *Vers pour être calomnié*, for example, with its deliberate matching of rhymes of different genders, seems to be purely ironic. *A la louange de Laure et de Pétrarque*, however, is both a parody and a celebration of the sonnet form. For the first quatrain's lyricism:

Chose italienne où Shakspeare [sic] a passé
Mais que Ronsard fit superbement française,
Fine basilique au large diocèse,
Saint-Pierre-des-Vers, immense et condensé . . .

becomes, in phrases like 'Saint-Pierre-des-Vers', touched with burlesque, whilst although in the second quatrain the sonnet is still seen to be

débout sous l'exégèse
Même edmondschéresque ou francisquesarceyse . . .

the long adjectives that swell out to fill the line again take the poem to the verge of parody.

Sonnet boiteux, on the other hand, is a piece of straight burlesque. Claude Cuénot quite misses the point of this tredecasyllabic joke when he asserts that:

le poète a voulu composer un sonnet aussi irrégulier que possible, surtout à la fin, pour donner à l'expression de sa douleur un pathétique tout à fait directe.'[11]

For the effect of this poem, in which an undistinguished irregular octave precedes a sestet whose rhyme-scheme becomes progressively tenuous ('Sohos'/'haôs') until in the second tercet it disappears altogether, is one that is not 'pathétique' but deliberately humorous in its effect. The anticipatory irony of the first quatrain, implying that the sonneteer himself is the 'naïf animal', suggests that the poet is poking fun both at his own emotion and at the form which gives it expression:

> Ah! vraiment c'est triste, ah! vraiment ça finit trop mal.
> Il n'est pas permis d'être à ce point infortuné.
> Ah! vraiment c'est trop la mort du naïf animal . . .

Verlaine's sonnet inspiration, even in the 1860s never particularly consistent, is thus by the 1880s even less firmly orientated. The religious sonnets of *Sagesse* are accomplished poems but their art is of a sort 'trop souvent réduit au métier acquis, extérieur à ce qu'il doit exprimer et que pour cette raison on peut admirer sans qu'on en soit touché'[12]. For the Verlainian sonnet no longer attempts to make creative discoveries: it tends to lapse, as we saw, either into an unquestioning acceptance of the form's contours or a rather crude modification of its surface details. The burlesque sonnets in *Jadis et naguère* sometimes lack subtlety and on the whole provide no real insight into the sonneteer's creative processes. These, however, are preferable to those sonnets composed out of convenience rather than real inspiration. Succumbing to a temptation that Mallarmé characteristically avoids, Verlaine in the *Dédicaces* (1890), addresses scores of occasional sonnets to his friends and contemporaries in which the sonnet form becomes merely a convenient *cadre* imposing an easily achieved elegance on an otherwise prosaic subject matter.

After the 1880s, Verlaine is a poet without theories. Unifying themes no longer impose order and coherence on his poetry, saving it from the gratuitousness sometimes evident in his later sonnets. Unlike Mallarmé, who, alone amongst poets of Verlaine's generation, was able to continue producing sonnets of the first order right into the 1890s[13], Verlaine reverts to a kind of *fin de siècle* romanticism in which:

> Le poète a fini sa tâche.
> L'homme, non.[14]

Such an attitude would have been impossible in a poet like Mallarmé, for a great sonneteer is conceivable only when the preoccupations of 'l'homme' and 'le poète' become synonymous. In the later

Verlaine this no longer seems to have been the case.

(ii) *Corbière*

The popularity of any literary form is almost invariably accompanied by its subjection to parody. Even at the height of its glory, the Elizabethan sonnet was susceptible to ironic attack. Shakespeare himself in *Love's Labour's Lost* has Holofernes, the pendant, dismiss the sonnet as mere arithmetical demonstration:

> Here are only numbers ratified . . .[1]

The nineteenth-century French sonnet was no exception to this rule. Already by the 1860s and 70s the formal liberties occasionally taken by a sonneteer like Mallarmé are accompanied by the veiled ironies noted in the preceding chapter. Verlaine's attitude towards the sonnet was, as we saw, in a different way ambiguous. It is Tristan Corbière however who most clearly illustrates the paradoxical situation of the sonneteer in the 1870s. On the one hand this poet, in poems like *I Sonnet*, subjects the form to the most overt and thorough ironic investigation of the century whilst, on the other, he has recourse to the form over thirty times in *Les Amours jaunes*.

At a superficial glance, Corbière's attitude appears to be that of a Romantic poet who, in the interests of greater freedom of expression, parodies the sonnet's strict formal demands. Some critics have confirmed this. Albert Sonnenfeld, for example, asserts that Corbière:

> insiste pour que l'émotion l'emporte sur la forme. Cette hostilité aux Parnassiens révèle combien l'anti-romantisme de Corbière est superficiel: sous son masque, il est aussi sentimental que l'auteur de *Graziella*[2].

Corbière's attitude towards the sonnet however is more subtle than this. For he is not, as Sonnenfeld suggests, a pure Romantic like Lamartine concealing himself behind a formal mask. On the contrary, he has a predilection for fixed forms that goes far beyond their scope as butts for parody and burlesque. His repeated use of the sonnet would seem to bear this out. If he had been a true Romantic, having once ironically and emphatically dismissed the sonnet, he would devote his energies to a different kind of poem and not keep on obsessively returning, as he does, to the type of forms that he has theoretically rejected.

When Ezra Pound, in his essay *Irony, Laforgue and some satire*, affirms that 'Verbalism demands a set form used with irreproachable skill. Satire needs, usually, the form of cutting rhymes to drive it home . . .'[3], these remarks become almost as appropriate to Corbière, who, moreover, is on several occasions mentioned in the essay. For set forms like the sonnet, whose close relationship with the epigram has been recognized in France since the sixteenth century[4], enhance the bite and concision of an ironic attitude. Baudelaire's mordant use of the octosyllabic sonnet in *Les Fleurs du Mal* is paralleled in the sonnets of *Les Amours jaunes,* sixteen of which use octosyllables (three in conjunction with either or both deca- and dodecasyllables). For just as the sonnet's special potential as a means of combining lyrical and romantic with analytical and ironical elements was noted in the context of Baudelaire, it is likewise exploited in Corbière's sonnets. In *Litanie,* for example, in the manner of Baudelaire's octosyllabic *Epigraphe pour un Livre condamné,* the poet's lyricism is allowed to expand not only through the octave but also deep into a feverish sestet until, only in the very last line, an ironic *volte-face* devastates the reader's expectations.

Corbière's use of the sonnet does not however always have the same flavour as that of Baudelaire. For coming one generation after the great mid-century poet, Corbière lived in a rather different poetic climate. Most of Baudelaire's sonnets were written in the early stages of the form's authentic nineteenth-century development, that is, in the 1840s and early 1850s, and the originality of Baudelaire partly lay in his ability to reach such a high degree of formal perfection so early. The sonnet did not reach the height of its vogue until the 1860s[5] when Verlaine and Mallarmé as well as Leconte de Lisle and Heredia were writing sonnets. Mallarmé's *Sonnet en '–yx'* (the first version of which was completed in 1868) reflects a refinement of attitude towards fixed forms that the more subtle and critical poets of the period were attempting to achieve. In *I Sonnet* (1873), Corbière's preoccupations were in many ways in line with these.

For Sonnenfeld, Corbière's *I Sonnet* is a simple reassertion of Romantic values after the decade of Parnassian formalism (1860–1870) that we have just mentioned. In the context of this 'attaque contre le formalisme' Sonnefeld declares that:

> Les Parnassiens ont réduit la poésie à une leçon de calligraphie et d'arithmétique, et les formes y remplacent l'inspiration véritable.[6]

This, and Sonnenfeld's assertion that 'Ecrire un poème est devenu un problème de calcul'[7] betray an oversimplified view of the matter. Because Corbière describes and analyses this 'problème de calcul' in the most ironic terms it does not necessarily follow that he rejects this attitude towards poetry. On the contrary, a more careful and detailed analysis of *I Sonnet* should give rise to a different idea of Corbière's attitude towards the sonnet.

Superficially of course, *I Sonnet* looks like a simple parody of the form:

I Sonnet
Avec la manière de s'en servir

Réglons notre papier et formons bien nos lettres:

Vers filés à la main et d'un pied uniforme,
Emboîtant bien le pas, par quatre en peloton;
Qu'en marquant la césure, un des quatre s'endorme . . .
Ça peut dormir debout comme soldats de plomb.

Sur le *railway* du Pinde est la ligne, la forme;
Aux fils de télégraphe: — on en suit quatre, en long;
A chaque pieu, la rime—exemple: *chloroforme.*
—Chaque vers est un fil, et la rime un jalon.

—Télégramme sacré—20 mots.—Vite à mon aide . . .
(Sonnet—c'est un sonnet—) ô Muse d'Archimède!
—La preuve d'un sonnet est par l'addition:

—Je pose 4 et 4 =8! Alors je procède,
En posant 3 et 3!—Tenons Pégase raide:
"O lyre! O délire! O . . ."—Sonnet—Attention!

The very presentation of the poem with its pseudo-reverent epigraph:

Réglons notre papier et formons bien nos lettres

emphasizes the sonneteer's self-consciousness as he smooths out his paper before committing himself to his consecrated task. The poetic ritual of sonnet-writing is accompanied by a strict set of rules which demand text-book elucidation. This Corbière ironically promises to provide in his first epigraph:

I Sonnet
Avec la manière de s'en servir

The first rule is the law of numbers. The sonneteer becomes Archimedes' Muse since the composition of a sonnet may basically be reduced to an arithmetical exercise:

> —Télégramme sacré—20 mots.—Vite à mon aide . . .
> (Sonnet—c'est un sonnet—) ô Muse d'Archimède!
> —La preuve d'un sonnet est par l'addition:
>
> —Je pose 4 et 4   8! Alors je procède,
> En posant 3 et 3 . . .

The ingenious railway imagery of the octave stresses another important rule: the 'télégramme sacré' must keep to the rails. Its lines are marshalled and regimented like lead soldiers whilst in the second quatrain, the lyrical 'filles du Pinde'—the Muses—board the *railway* du Pinde' and move into the regimented and industrialized world of the nineteenth century with its mathematical ideals and telegraph poles. Finally, the lead soldiers having successfully stamped any lyrical tendencies firmly underfoot, click obediently to a halt at the end of line 14:

> "O lyre! O délire! O . . ."—Sonnet—Attention!

The sonnet form's tyrannical laws are accompanied however by another proscription: the use of any rhyme-word that does not fit into the consecrated rhyme-scheme. Whereas Mallarmé, in the *Sonnet en '–yx'*, needing a fourth rhyme to complete the octave, was, as we saw, obliged to invent his own, Corbière's solution to this kind of problem is in a different way ironic. He selects any word, no matter how incongruous its meaning, provided it rhymes with its three other partners in the octave. Thus the rhymes 'uniforme', 's'endorme' and 'forme' are set off with:

> A chaque pieu, la rime—exemple: *chloroforme.*

It is in the sestet of the poem that the irony of the poet becomes intensified and refined. That *I Sonnet* is not a simple and spontaneous rejection of the sonnet form is borne out by Corbière's very subtle reference to an ironic tradition. For the sonnet does not suddenly, in the middle of the nineteenth century, become susceptible to parody but has, Corbière recognizes, always been so. Instead of Shakespeare's Holofernes, Corbière follows the example of a great comic writer of the seventeenth century like Molière who, through Oronte in *Le Misanthrope* (I, ii),, parodies the sonneteer who imagines he can automatically impose prestige on his verse by announcing:

> Sonnet—c'est un sonnet—

By picking up this ironic motif and blending into his own sonnet,

Corbière takes irony to the verge of self-parody. Furthermore, what gives this parody of the sonnet form its special quality, that lifts it above the game-playing that goes on in some of Verlaine's ironic sonnets, is the fact that Corbière is here meticulously, even ingeniously, obeying the rules he is satirizing. The content of the octave is patently suitable with its elaboration of theories on 'ligne', 'forme' and 'rime' whilst the shift into the sestet is, as it ought to be, a shift into a more concentrated register: the sestet becomes the 'télégramme sacré' that it evokes, adding up and expressing as a compact formula the figures of the octave.

Corbière's ironic attitude towards the sonnet was not thus, as it had sometimes been for the later Verlaine, a destructive one. Far from accepting the sonnet as an absolute form of poetic expression, Corbière is all too aware of its consecrated artificiality. But he does not, because of this, reject it out of hand. In the same way, Corbière's parody of rhyme in *I Sonnet* does not in any way prevent rhyme becoming for the poet an important source of poetic inspiration. The rhymes from Hugo's *Les Djinns,* for example, which had moreover, as we noted above, been used by idealizing sonneteers like Gautier and Baudelaire, which he burlesques in *A l'éternel Madame :*

Quand le poète brame en *Ame, en Lame, en Flamme!* . . .

he himself frequently exploits—as in *Le Poète contumace, Vendetta, A un Juvenal de lait, Idylle coupée* and on many other occasions.

It is not only the formal characteristics of the sonnet that Corbière parodies, for the traditional idealization of the poet's mistress is also given an ironic interpretation. In *Sonnet à Sir Bob,* composed in the unromantic setting of the 'British Channel', the lady's dog, and not the lady herself, is the subject of the poet's envious admiration. In the same way that in *I Sonnet,* Corbière parodies the formal rules he is himself meticulously obeying, in *Sonnet à Sir Bob* he parodies the emotional reponse to a loved object that he himself is experiencing.

In the sonnet *Le Crapaud,* a similar identity between man and animal is established but the system by which it is developed is reversed. Indeed, *Le Crapaud* is an inverted sonnet in more ways than one. Not only do the tercets precede the quatrains but also the metaphor that is at the core of the poem is fully developed before its significance is recognized by the reader. For only in the last line—

carefully separated from those that precede it—is the identity between poet and frog fully established.

Self-conscious on both formal and thematic levels, the Corbière of *Sonnet à Sir Bob* and *Le Crapaud* is a Romantic who uses the sonnet to burlesque his own romanticism whilst the Corbière of *I Sonnet* is a skilful formalist who uses the sonnet to parody his own Parnassian tendencies. Corbière is therefore a poet constantly aware of two diverging impulses. On the one hand, he adheres in his sonnets to the urbane, ironic Parisian tradition of Baudelaire, Verlaine and Mallarmé, with its self-conscious pre-occupation with refinement and fixed forms, whilst on the other hand he tries to infuse into them some of the energy and natural lyricism of the provincial poet that finds less self-conscious expression in the longer Breton poems like *Gens de mer*.

Corbière was perhaps the last important poet of the century, apart from Mallarmé, to write sonnets that do not, like those of the later Verlaine, Heredia, Samain or Valéry (to name but four) merely repeat, elegantly and gracefully perhaps, but mostly unoriginally, a given formula. For the vigour with which Corbière interrogated the sonnet form was a healthy phenomenon. It was the failure of subsequent poets to maintain this boldness in the exploitation of fixed forms like the sonnet that led to their decline —to, for example, Samain's mostly derivative sonnets—and to the rise of more vigorous prosaic forms like the *poème en prose* and *vers libre*.

(iii) *Laforgue*

In many ways Laforgue is the *fin de siècle* poet *par excellence*. Born in 1860, his poetry was written at a time when critics and literary historians were beginning to take stock of French Romantic poetry and place the most influential of its arbiters—Hugo, Leconte de Lisle and Baudelaire—in more definitive perspective. Laforgue's poetry reflects perhaps better than any other of the time, the self-consciousness and constraint of the poet toiling in the wake of a century's formal and thematic traditions.

For a sophisticated poet like Laforgue[1], as it had been to some degree for Verlaine, Mallarmé and even Corbière, the subject matter of nineteenth-century poetry after 1860 had largely been decided by Baudelaire. For the primeval impetus of the Romantic poet's empathy with Nature had to come to terms, after *Les Fleurs du Mal,* with the sophisticated logic of a city-orientated imagination. The themes of poetry became those susceptible to development by a complex, urban intellect : the self was no longer permitted to become unreservedly merged into the rhythms of an organic nature[2], the city poet too often catching his own reflection in the *brasserie* mirror or the café window to allow such unselfconsciousness. Irony therefore became an essential part of expressing the contrasts and complexities of the city poet's psyche. The structure of the sonnet, with its geometrical profile, its contrasts and antitheses, its tendency to fuse lyricism and logic and, above all, its leaning towards ironical self-analysis, proved to be for Baudelaire, as we saw, an ideal form of poetic expression.

In establishing some of the main preoccupations of later nineteenth-century French poetry, Baudelaire thus also indicated or confirmed the formal directions that it would take. Jasinski goes so far as to say that, after the 1860s, the sonnet's history and that of nineteenth-century French literature become almost synonymous[3]. Thus the formal preoccupations of the Symbolist generation of poets partly find their origin in the technical refinement demanded by forms like the sonnet. With Mallarmé, as we saw, these formal preoccupations become not only the basis but even the subject matter of poetry since, for him, a poem's composition becomes a question not so much of content as of arrangement.

This was also very much the case with Laforgue. In *Les Complaintes* (1885), most of the themes that dominate his later poetry — *L'Imitation de Notre-Dame la Lune, Des Fleurs de bonne volonté,* and *Derniers Vers*—are already established. Each following collection essentially consists of a fresh attempt to *arrange* or *compose* this established subject matter. Whole sections from the *Dimanches* poems of *Des Fleurs de bonne volonté,* for example, reappear, slightly rearranged, in the *Dimanches* of the *Derniers Vers.* Laforgue's creative life becomes thus one of a quest for the right form.

As far as this study is concerned, the most interesting formal transformation that Laforgue's poetry undergoes in this quest is that which takes place between *Le Sanglot de la terre,* his first, and, before his death, unpublished selection of verse, and *Les Com-*

plaintes, published, as we saw, in 1885, which really established his reputation amongst the poets of the Symbolist group.

In the sonnets of *Le Sanglot de la terre,* Laforgue takes the themes —pessimism and metaphysical anguish—of Baudelaire's later sonnets *(Le Couvercle, Le Gouffre),* and subjects them, or attempts to subject them, to a similar kind of development. Laforgue, however, still in his early twenties, has not yet refined his technique sufficiently to achieve the fine balance between emotion and irony that characterizes Baudelaire's mature sonnets. Indeed, *Le Sanglot de la terre,* as a whole, represents an attempt, never consistently realized, to achieve a synthesis of the diverging tendencies of the later nineteenth-century psyche. *La Première Nuit* and *Les Têtes de morts* are conscious or only semi-conscious pastiches of Baudelairian *macabre;* the epic romanticism of sonnets like *Intarissablement* and *Médiocrité* is unrelieved by irony whilst sonnets like *Méditation grisâtre* and *Farce éphémère* are not saved by the irony of their title from resounding bathos. *La Cigarette,* at the other end of the scale, however, is far more successful than any of these:

> Oui, ce monde est bien plat; quant à l'autre, sornettes.
> Moi, je vais résigné, sans espoir, à mon sort,
> Et pour tuer le temps, en attendant la mort,
> Je fume au nez des dieux de fines cigarettes.
>
> Allez, vivants, luttez, pauvres futurs squelettes.
> Moi, le méandre bleu qui vers le ciel se tord
> Me plonge en une extase infinie et m'endort
> Comme aux parfums mourants de mille cassolettes.
>
> Et j'entre au paradis, fleuri de rêves clairs
> Où l'on voit se mêler en valses fantastiques
> Des éléphants en rut à des chœurs de moustiques.
>
> Et puis, quand je m'éveille en songeant à mes vers,
> Je contemple, le cœur plein d'une douce joie,
> Mon cher pouce rôti comme une cuisse d'oie.

However, the nonchalant elegance and self-consciousness of this sonnet's style and the self-confident irony purify it of any deep emotion.

In these poems Laforgue is struggling, on the one hand, with the earnestness and grand epic preoccupations of the Romantics and, on the other, with the nonchalance and irony of the *fin de siècle* poet for whom subject matter or message are no longer primary considerations. Thus, in the latter group, as in a sonnet like *La*

Cigarette, the fantasizing poet's scorched thumb becomes no more arbitrary a choice of subject matter than the nature of the universe. Between these two extremes, however, there is one sonnet that really comes off, and that is *Apothéose:*

> En tous sens, à jamais, le Silence fourmille
> De grappes d'astres d'or mêlant leurs tournoiements.
> On dirait des jardins sablés de diamants,
> Mais, chacun, morne et très-solitaire, scintille.
>
> Or là-bas, dans un coin inconnu, qui pétille
> D'un sillon de rubis mélancoliquement,
> Tremblotte une étincelle au doux clignotement:
> Patriarche éclaireur conduisant sa famille.
>
> Sa famille: un essaim de globes lourds fleuris.
> Et sur l'un, c'est la terre, un point jaune, Paris,
> Où, pendue, une lampe, un pauvre fou qui veille:
>
> Dans l'ordre universel, frêle, unique merveille.
> Il en est le miroir d'un jour et le connaît.
> Il y rêve longtemps, puis en fait un sonnet.

This poem manages to convey within the formal structure of the sonnet both a late nineteenth-century attitude to form and a late nineteenth-century attitude to subject matter. The regular Petrarchan octave expresses a typical *fin de siècle* nihilism, the metaphysical anguish of the poet contemplating the universe. Note the already confident use of Mallarmean imagery—'astres', 'diamants', 'sillon de rubis', and also the neat reservation, through intricate organization of syntax, of the sparkling Mallarmean verb 'scintille' for the end of the first quatrain. Echoes of Victor Hugo are still perceptible in the second quatrain's imagery in which the sun is personified as:

> Patriarche éclaireur conduisant sa famille.

It is in the sestet however that is expressed the consciousness of disparity, not only between poet and universe, but between form and and subject. For step by step, in three rhyming couplets, the lyrical vision of the universe is telescoped into the act of writing a poem. Ll. 11 and 12 are most suggestively coupled, juxtaposing the initial self-conscious thrust of the cynic:

> Où pendue, une lampe, un pauvre fou qui veille

and the idealizing tendencies of the lyrical poet:

> Dans l'ordre universel, frêle, unique merveille.

And finally, the penultimate line, the perfect image of the late nineteenth-century poet's self-consciousness:

> Il en est le miroir d'un jour et le connaît

is juxtaposed with the idealization, both ludicrous and poignant, of the last line:

> Il y rêve longtemps, puis en fait un sonnet.

Laforgue's technique of endstopping every line of the sestet, four of them on a full stop, is more generally significant in the context of the use of the sonnet by Corbière, Verlaine and Laforgue himself. For the fundamental problem of all these poets was how to combine in one poem two radically opposed elements: ironic self-analysis and naive lyricism. In Verlaine, as we saw, the two were seldom satisfactorily blended: two different attitudes are given parallel development but there never seems to be a point at which the parallels converge. In the Laforgue of *Apothéose,* the parallels have come very close together: l. 11 expresses a diametrically opposite attitude to l. 12, and l. 13 to l. 14, but the nearer the sonnet draws to its close, the closer the two parallels become. The result of this is that in the final couplet, each line contains elements of both an ironic and a lyrical nature:

> Il en est le miroir d'un jour [lyrical]
>   et le connaît [ironic]
> Il y rêve longtemps [lyrical]
>   puis en fait un sonnet [ironic]

Despite the success (in our view) of *Apothéose,* there are, after *Le Sanglot de la terre,* virtually no more sonnets in Laforgue. What was the reason for this? In fact the seeds of Laforgue's abandonment of the sonnet are already sown in *Le Sanglot de la terre* in which, as we have just seen, both the metaphysical and the sophisticated tendencies of the *fin de siècle* sonnet are beginning to be parodied. *Apothéose,* for example, sends up not only the Baudelairian metaphysical sonnet but also that of Mallarmé, it being a kind of burlesque of poems like *Ses purs ongles* ... Similarly, *La Cigarette* provides an ironical interpretation of a theme explored in Baudelaire's sonnets like *La Pipe* and in Mallarmé's *Toute l'âme résumée* ...., although the composition of Laforgue's poem precedes that of the latter by over a decade.

It is here that Laforgue's irony becomes symptomatic of a more general dissatisfaction with the sonnet—not only in himself but also in other later nineteenth-century poets. Already in 1882 Laforgue admits to having lost 'le préjugé du sonnet'[4] whilst Verhaeren comments:

> Le bon sonnet, tant loué par Boileau, mais il croît aujourd'hui comme de l'herbe le long des routes, et tout âne académique peut en brouter et s'en remplir la panse![5]

For by the end of the century, the sonnet is no longer the fresh and promising poetic form that it had been to Gautier, Nerval and Baudelaire. After fifty years of development, or perhaps over-development, its resources were nearing exhaustion. Now the *fin de siècle* poet wanted at all costs to escape merely re-echoing the stylistic or thematic moves of his immediate predecessors. Unlike Verlaine however, Laforgue wisely resists the temptation of playing with the sonnet's formal profile. In this he follows Gautier's dictum, already quoted, that recommended either a total acceptance of the sonnet's formal rules or their total rejection. And this is what Laforgue does. Out of the twelve sonnets in *Le Sanglot de la terre,* all but one *(La Première Nuit)* have a regular octave in *abba abba* and all but four a regular sestet in *ccd ede* or *ccd eed.* When however the short-comings of the sonnet become clear to Laforgue, he simply stops using the form. By largely abandoning the sonnet after *Le Sanglot de la terre* therefore, Laforgue takes the first step, and an important one, towards avoiding the undesirable nineteenth-century echoes that by now it inevitably brings with it.

Part of Laforgue's originality thus lies in his realization, after about 1885, that the sonnet is no longer for him a valid poetic form. Unlike the later Verlaine, Samain and the early Valéry, he never succumbs to the temptation of its elegance, nostalgia and prestige. Following Corbière's example, he no longer unquestioningly accepts the sonnet or any other fixed form. In this Laforgue's short poetic career becomes in some ways the blue-print for the late nineteenth-century or early twentieth-century poet, in which an early acceptance of the sonnet, following the great Symbolist poets' example, is soon superseded as, under the influence of Corbière and Verlaine, his poetry progressively evolves through *vers libéré* to *vers libre.* It was ultimately only into the latter that Laforgue, the *fin de siècle* poet, was able to escape his great nineteenth-century predecessors and create an original contribution to his nation's poetry.

CONCLUSION

It is a paradox that after the 1860s and 70s, when, as we saw, the sonnet was at the height of its vogue, its essential creative role was becoming undermined. Perhaps it was its very popularity that, leading to over-exploitation and stereotyping, made any unified trend of development an impossibility. The publication in 1875 of *Le Livre des sonnets,* accompanied by a reprint of Charles Asselineau's *Histoire du sonnet pour servir à l'histoire de la poésie française* of 1855, confirmed the tendency, established in the 1860s, towards the sonnet's vulgarization. The special integrity of the Baudelairian sonnet was never, except by Mallarmé, equalled by other poets, Samain, and even on occasion, Verlaine, Cros, Corbière, Laforgue, plundering the great mid-century sonneteer for rhymes and themes. Mallarmé's sonnets, with their formal perfection, their infallible poise and deep suggestiveness, alone, after 1875, constitute a development of the form that was both stable and original. The ironic attitude towards the sonnet[1], prefigured by Nerval, present in Baudelaire, subtle and salutary in Mallarmé, still beneficial in Corbière, becomes destructive in Verlaine and leads finally, with Laforgue, to the rejection of the form.

When in the *Illuminations* Rimbaud calls part of his prose poem *Jeunesse* of 1874[2] *Sonnet,* he prefigures the loss of prestige that the sonnet will suffer in the last quarter of the nineteenth century in France[3]. For the sonnet was no longer accepted by the *avant garde* poets of this period as a consecrated form. The paroxysm of self-consciousness that these latter poets experienced at this time— Laforgue with his theory of *l'inconscient* and Rimbaud with his *dérèglement* de *tous les sens'*—inevitably had its repercussions in the formal sphere. Anticipating the Surrealists, they felt, after nearly a century of poetic refinement and sophistication, a fresh desire to escape into the unconsciousness of *l'informe.* The latter's disorganization and disarray coming as a distinct relief after 50 years of fixed forms, found its expression in the *vers libre* and the *poème en prose* that were to provide the most invigorating source of late nineteenth-century French poetry.

The fact that after the 1880s there were no more major sonnets on the sonnet is also perhaps symptomatic of the decline in sonnet inspiration and the falling off of interest in the form's expressive possibilities. Valéry's attempt to revive or rather maintain the sonnet as a valid poetic medium was neither energetic nor convincing enough to reverse this downward trend. It is unfair perhaps to criticize *L'Album de vers anciens* for its lack of originality: like other sonneteers of the nineties (Louÿs, Samain, Régnier), Valéry was almost inevitably very much influenced by Mallarmé and Heredia and critics generally agree[4] on the almost entirely derivative and reminiscent nature of the early poems. Unfortunately however, the deep research that Valéry claims to have devoted to the sonnet since Petrarch, began around 1910 and continued intermittently through the First World War, seems to have borne remarkably little fruit in the poems of *Charmes* (1922). There are only 6 sonnets in the entire collection (Valéry's total output of sonnets, including those in the *Album* and his occasional pieces, being doubled even by that of Mallarmé), and the special importance Valéry theoretically attached to the quadruple rhyme of the classical octave appears scarcely to influence, in practice, his use of the sonnet in *Charmes*. Although he declares that:

> Les mêmes rimes aux quatrains ont une signification qu'il faut trouver. *Faire le sonnet, c'est trouver cette signification*—c'est trouver une des expressions ou solutions de cette relation, *mêmes rimes*. (Un bon sonnet ferait sentir qu'il *fallait* que les deux quatrains rimassent entre eux.)[5]

in fact only two of the six sonnets in *Charmes, L'Abeille* and *La Dormeuse*, attempt to express this magical 'relation, *mêmes rimes*'. Indeed, one of the characteristics of the sonnets in *Charmes* is their irregulairty—only *La Dormeuse* being an entirely regular sonnet. In spite of the long research and deep reflection that he devoted to the sonnet, *Charmes* reveal a Valéry far more at home in the long poem.[6]

The rise and fall of the sonnet in the seventy years between 1829 and 1900 coincided with a period of the most intensive poetic activity in France since the Renaissance. Indeed, the nineteenth-century sonnet is in many ways as important and influential as that of the sixteenth century from which it derives. Like Du Bellay and Ronsard, Baudelaire and Mallarmé created a radically new kind of poetry in which, as we have tried to show, the sonnet played a crucial role. For it is doubtful whether the revolution that converted the language of French poetry after the 1830s and 40s from the discursive and narrative verse of the Romantics into the imaged and concentrated medium of the Symbolists could have been achieved without the sonnet. In tracing the development—theoretical and practical—of the latter throughout the nineteenth century we have, therefore, tried to show how the sonnet's peculiar ability to unite precision and suggestiveness, formal perfection and imaginative depth, lyricism and self-consciousness, enabled it to become a phenomenon of fundamental importance in the development of nineteenth-century French poetry.

INTRODUCTION

1 Recently reprinted by Slatkine (Geneva, 1968).

2 Karl Schofer's more recent short unpublished thesis called *Baudelaire the Son-neteer* (Princeton, 1970), though modernising and correcting certain misconceptions in Cassagne's study, is itself so fraught with errors and misconceptions about fundamentals—such as the nature of rhyme in French—as scarcely to provide a satisfactory replacement for the earlier work.

3 *Australian Journal of French Studies*, 6, (1969), p. 331.

4 By 'Symbolist' I mean those poets who, following Nerval and Baudelaire, use the sonnet not so much as a framework for descriptive or discursive developments, but exploit its structure as a means of exploring deeper psychological tendencies or other, less rationally definable but none the less coherent, patterns of meaning. (I hope this distinction will become clear in the sections on Nerval and Baudelaire). Hereafter, I shall use the terms 'Symbolist' and 'Parnassian' without inverted commas.

5 'Valéry et la tradition du sonnet français et européen', *Entretiens sur Paul Valéry* (Paris, Presses Universitaires de France, 1972), p. 165.

6 For example, H. Vaganay's *Le Sonnet en Italie et en France au 16e siècle* (2 vols., Lyon, Au Siège des Facultés Catholiques, 1902–3), and, for 16th & 17th C. sonnet developments, see Jasinski, op. cit., pp. 32–154.

7 Recent research has favoured Marot or Jean Boucher as the French originator, see C. A. Mayer: 'Le premier sonnet français: Marot, Mellin de Saint-Gelais, et Jean Boucher', *Revue d'Histoire Littéraire de la France*, 67 (1967), pp. 481–93 and 'Gabriele Simeoni et le premier sonnet français', *Studi Francesi*, XVIII, 53 (1974), pp. 213–23.

8 See Jasinski, op. cit., pp. 7–31.

CHAPTER I

1 Boileau: *Art poétique*, Chant II, 1.94, in *Œuvres* (ed. Mongrédien, Paris, Garnier, 1961), p. 168.

2 Keats: *The Fall of Hyperion*, 1.445.

3 Op. cit., p. 193.

4 *Traité général de versification française* (Paris, Charpentier, 1879), p. 62.

5 *Prosodie de l'école moderne* (Paris, Didier, 1844), p. 84.

6 *Tableau de la poésie française au XVIe siècle* (Paris, Lemerre, 1876, first published 1828), II, p. 88.

7 *Préface des œuvres choisies de Pierre de Ronsard* (1828) in the *Tableau*, II, p. 404.

8 *Tableau*, I, p. 202.

9 *Les Œuvres et les hommes*, III, ix (Geneva, Slatkine Reprints, 1968), p. 177.

10 The nineteenth-century English tradition of sonnets on the sonnet continuing through Rossetti and even through minor *fin de siècle* poets like Lord Alfred Douglas.

11 *The Metres of English Poetry* (London, Methuen, 1969), pp. 206–207.

12 Nerval at this time was showing a similar interest in Renaissance sonneteers like Ronsard and Du Bartas, he re-editing the Pléiade poets in 1830, these latter having a far more enriching influence on Nerval's sonnets than on those of Sainte-Beuve however.

13 *L'Évolution de la poésie lyrique en France au dix-neuvième siècle* (Paris, Hachette, 1895), p. 252.

14 *Anthologie de la poésie française* (Pléiade, Paris, Gallimard, 1949), p. 23.

15 *Œuvres complètes* (Pléiade, Paris, Gallimard, 1961), p. 199.

16 *Baudelaire* (Paris, Mercure de France, 1964), p. 267.

CHAPTER II
1 'Baudelaire' in *Souvenirs romantiques* (Paris, Garnier, 1929), p. 313.
2 Ibid., p. 315.
3 *Dernières Poésies*, in *Poésies complètes*, III (Ed. Jasinski, Paris, Nizet, 1970), pp. 272–283.
4 Ibid., pp. 281 and 293.
5 cf. E. Bergerat, *T. Gautier, entretiens, souvenirs et correspondances* (Paris, Charpentier, 1879), pp. 98–9.
6 *Poésies diverses* in *Poésies complètes*, II, op. cit., pp. 51–251.
7 Those few sonnets having a sestet in two rhymes only are included in the regular group.
8 Léopold Dauphin, *Regards en arrière*, (Beziers, 1912), p. 21.
9 Editor of Gautier's *Poésies complètes*, 3 vols. (Paris, Nizet, 1970), here cited in this work's Introduction, vol. I, p. LXXXIII.
10 Ibid., pp. CXXXIX–CXL.
11 'Sur les sonnets d'Ev. Boulay-Paty', *Presse*, 28 juillet 1851, cited by Jasinski, ibid., p. CXLIII.
12 An exactly contrary idea being expressed by Verlaine at about the same time in his *Art poétique* (1874) in which he exclaims: 'O qui dira les torts de la Rime?'
13 *Petit traité de poésie française* (Paris, Charpentier, 1922), pp. 199–200.
14 'La vie comparée de deux formes: le sonnet et le rondeau' in *Stil- und Formprobleme in der Literatur* (Ed. Paul Böckmann, Heidelberg, Winter, 1959), p. 105.
15 Op. cit., p. 202.
16 *Correspondance générale*, III, (Ed. Crépet, Paris, Conard, 1948), 504, p. 45.
17 For Barbey d'Aurevilly, see Chapter I and for J. Lemaître, his article 'Joséphin Soulary' in *Études et portraits littéraires*, III (Paris, Lecène Oudin, 1896), pp. 169-87.
18 Cited by F. Brunot and Ch. Bruneau in their *Précis de grammaire historique de la langue française* (Paris, Masson, 1949), p. 586.
19 *Œuvres* IV (Paris, Lemerre, 1860), pp. 248–49.
20 Their sonnets did not appear in *Le Parnasse contemporain* of 1866 though poems by Soulary were to figure in the later two volumes.
21 'Le sonnet de Baudelaire et la poésie anglaise', *Revue Germanique*, V (1909), p. 596.
22 Ibid.

CHAPTER III (i)
1 *Œuvres* I (Ed. J. Bailbé, Paris, Didier, 1967), pp. 290–91, the rhymes in '–onnet' of this sonnet's first quatrain being 'Simonnet' and 'bonnet'.
2 Cited in P. Guiraud's *Essais de stylistique* (Paris, Klincksieck, 1969), p. 249.
3 *Œuvres* I (Ed. A. Béguin and J. Richer, Pléiade, Paris, Gallimard, 1966), p. 158.
4 For a fuller analysis of these developments, see, for example, Albert S. Gérard, 'Images, structure et thèmes dans *El Desdichado'*, *Modern Language Review*, LVII, no. 4 (1963), pp. 507–15.
5 'Langage et race chez Nerval', *Cahiers du Sud*, 331, 1955, p. 366.
6 A. G. Engstrom 'The *Horus* of Gérard de Nerval', *Philological Quarterly*, XXXIII, no. I (1954), p. 80.
7 *La Poésie depuis Baudelaire* (Paris, Colin, 1965), p. 17.
(ii)
1 Op. cit., p. 9.
2 *Œuvres complètes* (Ed. Y.–G. Le Dantec & Co. Pichois, Pléiade, Paris, Gallimard, 1961), p. 359.

3 Op. cit., p. 175.
4 *La Genèse d'un poème*, in *Traductions, Œuvres complètes* (Ed. Crépet, Paris, Conard, 1965), p. 153. It was also, of course, in Poe's *Philosophy of Composition* that Baudelaire found a full theoretical justification for the short poem and a discussion of the advantages of placing 'distinct limits' on the poem's length.
5 Lettre à A. Fraisse, 18 février 1860, *Correspondance générale*, III, p. 39.
6 *Œuvres complètes* (Pléiade), p. 1261.
7 Lettre à De Calonne, 8 janvier 1859, *Correspondance générale*, II, 405, p. 256.
8 Lettre à Fraisse, 18 février 1860, op. cit., III, p. 40.
9 R. Vivier, *L'Originalité de Baudelaire* (Brussels, Palais des Académies, 1952), p. 71.
10 Jasinski, op. cit., pp. 7–31.
11 Italics mine in last eight sonnets quoted.
12 *Baudelaire* (Paris, Mercure de France, 1964), p. 19.
13 *Fusées, Œuvres complètes* (Pléiade), p. 1256.
14 Op. cit., p. 196.
15 Op. cit., pp. 13–14.
16 *Fusées*, VIII, op. cit., p. 1254,
17 *Correspondance générale*, V, 1007, p. 313.
18 Ibid., III, 502, pp. 39–40.
19 Cf. J. A. Scott, 'Petrarch and Baudelaire', *Revue de Littérature Comparée*, XXI, 4 (1957), pp. 550–562.
20 L. J. Austin in his article 'Mallarmé disciple de Baudelaire: Le Parnasse contemporain', *Revue d'Histoire Littéraire de la France*, 67 (1967), pp. 437–449, outlines certain aspects of Baudelaire's influence on Mallarmé at this period, especially those connected with phraseology and metaphorical developments.
21 *Parnasse et symbolisme* (Paris, Colin, 1925), p. 85.
(iii)
1 Those, that is, wirtten after 1862–5, in which the Baudelairian influence sketched at the end of the preceding section, had worn off.
2 Lettre à Cazalis, novembre 1864, *Correspondance*, I, lxiv, p. 137.
3 *Œuvres complètes* (Ed. H. Mondor & G. Jean-Aubry, Pléiade, Paris, Gallimard, 1965), p. 368.
4 Op. cit., p. 47.
5 The earlier sonnet is reproduced in the notes of the Pléiade edition of Mallarmé's *Œuvres complètes*, p. 1488, and both versions of the sonnet are given comprehensive treatment in, for example, R. Fromilhague's 'Nouvelle exégèse d'un sonnet de Mallarmé', *Littératures* III (1953), pp. 2186. Other important or controversial exegeses of this sonnet will be included in the bibliography.
6 18 juillet 1868, *Correspondance*, I, cxli, p. 278.
7 'Mallarmé's Ptyx Sonnet: an analytical and critical study', *Publications of the Modern Language Association of America*, 1950, pp. 75–89.
8 *Œuvres complètes*, p. 136.
9 *Correspondance*, I, cxxxviii, p. 274.
10 Lettre à Cazalis, op. cit., p. 279.
11 'Du sonnet', *Les Lettres Françaises*, 506, 4 mars 1954.
12 Mai 1867, *Correspondance*, I, cxxii, p. 243.
13 *L'Expression littéraire dans l'œuvre de Mallarmé* (Geneva, Droz, 1947), p. 144.
14 Juin 1862, *Correspondance*, I, x, p. 32.

CHAPTER IV (i)

1 *Les Hommes d'aujourd'hui* (1885–1893), *Œuvres en prose complètes* (Ed. Borel, Pléiade, Paris, Gallimard, 1972), p. 863.

2 Ibid.

3 Ibid.

4 This flexibility is reflected in *Romances sans paroles,* published in 1874, each of the twenty-three poems in this collection presenting, according to P. Guiraud in his study of them, 'une forme unique et originale fondée sur quelque variation de la mesure, de la rime ou de la strophe', *Essais de stylistique* (Paris, Klincksieck, 1969), p. 265.

5 Charles Cros in *Le Collier de griffes* (composed in the 1880s though not published until 1908, 20 years after the poet's death) follows Verlaine's example here. In his *Quatorze vers à Victor Hugo,* a quatrain of masculine follows a quatrain of feminine rhymes whilst, furthermore, in the sonnet's sestet, a tercet of feminine is followed by a tercet of masculine rhymes. In other sonnets of this period Cros displays even greater virtuosity: in *Pluriel féminin,* for example, as the title suggests, the entire sonnet is constructed around four feminine rhymes.

6 Cf. J.–P. Richard's 'Fadeur de Verlaine' in *Poésie et profondeur* (Paris, Editions du Seuil, 1955), pp. 165–185, and O. Nadal's *Paul Verlaine* (Paris, Mercure de France, 1961).

7 Nadal, op. cit., p. 66; Richard, op. cit., p. 181; E. Zimmermann, *Magies de Verlaine: étude de l'évolution poétique de Paul Verlaine* (Paris, Corti, 1967), p. 205.

8 Ibid.

9 Ibid., p. 151.

10 *L'Impressionisme français* (Geneva, Droz, 1952), p. 242.

11 *Le Style de Paul Verlaine* (Paris, Centre de la Documentation Universitaire, 1962), p. 470.

12 Zimmermann, op. cit., p. 205.

13 As was Heredia, whose *Trophées* appeared in 1893.

14 *Le Livre posthume, Œuvres poétiques complètes* (Ed. Le Dantec, Pléiade, Paris, Gallimard, 1954), p. 816.

(ii)

1 IV, ii, l. 113 in the Alexander edition of *The Complete Works of Shakespeare* (London, Collins, 1971), p. 180.

2 *L'Œuvre poétique de Tristan Corbière* (Paris, Presses Universitaires de France, 1960), p. 142.

3 *Literary Essays* (London, Faber, 1954), p. 283.

4 The seventeenth-century theorist G. Colletet, for example, in his *Traité du sonnet* (1658), sees the sonnet as being an 'épigramme bornée d'un certain nombre de Vers', *L'Art poétique* (Geneva, Droz, 1965), p. 124.

5 Cf. Jasinski, op. cit., p. 207.

6 Op. cit., p. 141.

7 Ibid.

(iii)

1 Whom Ezra Pound called 'perhaps the most sophisticated of all the French poets', op. cit., p. 281.

2 The more Romantic Rimbaud is perhaps an exception to this rule.

3 Op. cit., p. 251.

4 'Notes sur Baudelaire' in *Mélanges posthumes* (Paris, Mercure de France, 1913), p. 115.

5 'Jean Moréas' in *Impressions,* III (Paris, Mercure de France, 1928), p. 124. See also 'Le Nouveau Sonnet' of Louis Veuillot (1813–1883) which appears in F. Gregh's *Sonnets d'hier et d'aujourd'hui* (Paris, Tiranty, 1949), p. 116.

CONCLUSION

1 Also evident in *Les Déliquescences* (1885) of 'Adoré Floupette' (Henri Beauclair & Gabriel Vicaire), in which both the form and content of the later nineteenth-century sonnet are parodied in *Platonisme, Avant d'entrer, Sonnet libertin,* and *Décadents.*
2 This date established by A. Py in his edition of the *Illuminations* (Geneva, Droz, 1967).
3 Barbey d'Aurevilly had also written a prose poem entitled *Sonnet* as early as 1854, cf. *Rythmes oubliés* (Paris, Lemerre, 1897).
4 Cf. A. E. Mackay, *The Universal Self: A Study of Paul Valéry* (London, Routledge, 1961), p. 47 and A. W. Thomson, *Valéry* (London, Oliver and Boyd, 1965) p. 7.
5 *Cahiers,* 8, p. 357, cited in J. R. Lawler's *Lecture de Valéry: une étude de 'Charmes'* (Paris, Presses Universitaires de France, 1963), p. 25.
6 Although space here does not allow further discussion of Valéry's sonnet theory and practice, other works treating the subject may nevertheless be found in the bibliography of this study.

A SELECT BIBLIOGRAPHY

I The Sonnet
Aragon, Louis, 'Du sonnet', *Les Lettres Françaises,* 506, 4 mars 1954
Asselineau, Charles, *Histoire du sonnet pour servir à l'histoire de la poésie française,* Alençon, 1855.
Banville, Théo. de, 'Le Sonnet' in *Petit traité de poésie française,* Paris, Charpentier, 1922 (first pub., 1872).
Colletet, Guillaume, 'Traité du sonnet' in *Art poétique I,* Geneva, Droz, 1965 (first pub., Paris, 1658).
Elwert, W. Th., 'Sonnet' in *Traité de versification française des origines à nos jours,* Paris, Klincksieck, 1965, pp. 177–84.
Fuller, John, *The Sonnet,* The Critical Idiom, London, Methuen, 1972.
Jasinski, Max, *Histoire du sonnet en France,* Douai, Brugère et Dalsheimer, 1903.
Mitlacher, Heinz, *Moderne Sonnetgestaltung,* Leipzig, Noske, 1932.
Mönch, W., *Das Sonnet, Gestalt und Geschichte,* Heidelberg, Kerle, 1955.
Morier, Henri, 'Sonnet' in *Dictionnaire de poétique et de rhétorique,* Paris, Presses Universitaires de France, 1961, pp. 381–96.
Zaleski, Z. L., 'La Vie comparée de deux formes, le sonnet et le rondeau', in *Stil- und Formprobleme in der Literatur,* (Ed. P. Böckmann), Heidelberg, Winter, 1959, pp. 103–7.

II Some Sonnet Collections and a Representative Choice of Collections including Sonnets by Individual Poets.
Le Parnasse contemporain (3 vols.), Paris, Lemerre, 1866, 1869–71, 1876.
Le Livre des sonnets, Paris, Lemerre, 1875.
Sonnets d'hier et d'aujourd'hui (Ed. F. Gregh), Paris, Tiranty, 1949.
Banville, Théo. de, *Les Cariatides* (1842), *Rimes dorées* (1863–90) and *Le Sang de la coupe* (1846–79) in *Œuvres,* IX vols., Geneva, Slatkine, 1972.

Barbier, Auguste, *Rimes héroïques*, Paris, Masgana, 1843.

Brizeux, Auguste, *Histoires poétiques* in *Œuvres complètes, II*, Paris, Michel Lévy, 1860.

Corbière, Tristan, *Les Amours jaunes* in *Œuvres complètes* (Ed. Forestier & Walzer), Pléiade, Paris, Gallimard, 1970.

Cros, Charles, *Le Coffret de santal* & *Le Collier de griffes* in *Œuvres complètes* (Ed. Forestier & Walzer), Pléiade, Paris, Gallimard, 1970.

Gautier, Théophile, *Poésies complètes* (Ed. R. Jasinski, 3 vols.), Paris, Nizet, 1970.

Heredia, José-Maria de, *Les Trophées*, Paris, 1893.

Laforgue, Jules, *Le Sanglot de la terre* in *Poésies complètes* (Ed. Pia), Livre de Poche, Paris, Gallimard, 1971.

Leconte de Lisle, *Poèmes barbares*, Paris, 1862–1872.

Mallarmé, Stéphane, *Poësies* (1887) in *Œuvres complètes* (Ed. Mondor & Jean-Aubry), Pléiade, Paris, Gallimard, 1965.

Musset, Alfred de, *Poésies complètes* (Ed. Allem), Pléiade, Paris, Gallimard, 1957.

Nerval, Gérard de, *Les Chimères* in *Œuvres I* (Ed. Béguin & Richer), Pléiade, Paris, Gallimard, 1960.

Sainte-Beuve, C.-A., *Poésies de Joseph Delorme, Les Consolations, Pensées d'août*, Paris, Charpentier, 1890 (first pub., 1829, 1830 and 1837 respectively).

Samain, Albert, *Au jardin de l'infante* (1893) in *Œuvres I*, Paris, Editions d'Art H. Piazza, n.d.

Soulary, Joséphin, *Sonnets humoristiques*, Paris, Lemerre, 1858.

Valéry, Paul, *Album de vers anciens & Charmes* in *Œuvres I* (Ed. Hytier), Pléiade, Paris, Gallimard, 1957.

Verlaine, Paul, *Poèmes saturniens & Sagesse* in *Œuvres poétiques complètes* (Ed. Le Dantec & Borel), Pléiade, Paris, Gallimard, 1962.

III Studies on individual poets that deal with the Sonnets

(i) BAUDELAIRE

Cassagne, Albert, *Versification et métrique de Ch. Baudelaire*, Paris, Hachette, 1906.

Gautier, Théophile, 'Baudelaire' in *Souvenirs romantiques*, Paris, Garnier, 1929, pp. 262–341.

Potez, Henri, 'Les Sonnets de Baudelaire et la poésie anglaise', *Revue germanique* (1909), pp. 589–98.

Prévost, Jean, *Baudelaire*, Paris, Mercure de France, 1964 (first pub., 1953).

Rat, Maurice, 'Oiseaux charmants les rimes...Baudelaire', *Vie et langage*, 96 (1960), pp. 139–44.

Scott, J. A., 'Petrarch and Baudelaire', *Revue de Littérature Comparée*, XXXI (1957). pp. 550–62.

(ii) MALLARME

Abastado, Claude, 'Lecture inverse d'un sonnet nul', *Littérature*, 6 (1972), pp. 78–85.

Chassé, Charles, *Les Clés de Mallarmé*, Aubier, Editions Montaigne, 1954.

Chisholm, A. R., *Mallarmé's 'Grand Œuvre'*, Manchester, The University Press, 1962.

Chisholm, A. R., 'Mallarmé : Ses purs ongles...', *French Studies*, VI (1952), pp. 230–4.

Chisholm, A. R., 'Mallarmé and the riddle of the Ptyx', *Australian Universities Modern Language Association*, 40 (1973), pp. 246–8.

Citron, Pierre, Sur le sonnet en YX de Mallarmé', *Revue d'Histoire Littéraire de la France*, 69 (1969), pp. 113–16.

Davies, Gardner, *Les 'Tombeaux' de Mallarmé*, Paris, Corti, 1950.

Dragonetti, Roger, 'La Littérature et la lettre (Introduction au *Sonnet en X* de Mallarmé)', *Lingua e stile*, 4 (1969), pp. 205-22.

Fromilhague, R., 'Nouvelle exégèse d'un sonnet de Mallarmé', *Littératures*, II (1953), pp. 218-36.

Gay-Crozier, R., 'Le Sonnet en YX de Stéphane Mallarmé', *Culture*, 1967, pp. 285-92.

Grubbs, H. A., 'Mallarmé's ptyx' sonnet: an analytical and critical study', *Publications of the Modern Language Association of America*, 1950, pp. 75-89.

Kromer, Gretchen, 'The redoubtable PTYX', *Modern Language Notes*, 1971, pp. 563-72.

Nelson, R. J., 'Mallarmé's Mirror of Art. An explication of *Ses purs ongles...*, *Modern Language Quarterly*, 1959, pp. 49-56.

Noulet, Emilie, *Vingt poèmes de Stéphane Mallarmé*, Geneva, Droz, 1967.

Sewel, Elizabeth, 'Mallarmé and the world of the sonnets' in *The Structure of Modern Poetry*, London, Routledge, 1951, pp. 136-58.

Thibaudet, Albert, *La Poésie de Stéphane Mallarmé*, Paris, Gallimard, 1926.

Williams, T. A., 'Mallarmé's *Plusieurs sonnets*, IV', *Explicator*, XXV (1966), 28.

(iii) NERVAL

Gérard, Albert S., 'Images, structure et thèmes dans *El Desdichado*', *Modern Language Review*, LVIII (1963), pp. 507-15.

Kneller, John, 'The Poet and his Moira: *El Desdichado*', *Publications of the Modern Language Association of America*, LXXV (1960), pp. 402-9.

Le Hir, Yves, 'La Versification de Gérard de Nerval', *Lettres romanes*, X (1956), pp. 409-22.

Meschonnic, Henri, 'Essai sur la poétique de Nerval', *Europe*, 353 (1958), pp. 10-33.

Pellegrin, Jean, 'Commentaire sur *El Desdichado*', *Cahiers du sud*, 387-8, (1966), pp. 276-95.

Richer, Jean, *Nerval, expérience et création*, Paris, Hachette, 1963.

Rinsler, Norma, *Les Chimères* (Edition), London, Athlone, 1973.

(iv) VALERY

Guiraud, Pierre, *Langage et versification d'après l'œuvre de Paul Valéry*, Paris, Klincksieck, 1953.

Hytier, Jean, *La Poétique de Valléry*, Paris, Colin, 1970.
'L'Esthétique valéryenne du sonnet', *Australian Journal of French Studies*, 6 (1969), pp. 326-36.

Lawler, James R., *Lecture de Valéry: une étude de 'Charmes,'* Paris, Presses Universitaires de France, 1963.

Mönch, Walter, 'Valéry et la tradition du sonnet français et européen' in *Entretiens sur Paul Valéry. Actes du Colloque de Montpellier, 1971* (Ed. D. Moutote), Paris, Presses Universitaires de France, 1972, pp. 157-72.

(v) VERLAINE

Cuénot, Claude, *Le Style de Paul Verlaine*, Paris, Centre de la Documentation Universitaire, 1962.

Zimmermann, E. M., *Magies de Verlaine: étude de l'évolution poétique de Paul Verlaine*, Paris, Corti, 1967.

CORRECTION

The inside back cover should read as follows:—

UNIVERSITY OF HULL

OCCASIONAL PAPERS IN MODERN LANGUAGES

This series is intended to consist of studies, both literary and linguistic, relating to all principal European languages written in the main by members of the modern language departments in the University of Hull.

Obtainable through booksellers, or from the Secretary, The Publications Committee, The University, Hull, HU6 7RX